To Mr + Mrs Julius Livingston

In friendship
and highest esteem,
with every fond wish
and fondest memories
of our being together
in Israel.

Sam Goldfarb

Sarasota
Nov 25, 1964

# HOW FROM A MONKEY I BECAME A MAN

# HOW FROM A MONKEY I BECAME A MAN

SAM GOLDFARB

LIBRARY OF CONGRESS CATALOG CARD NUMBER 64–22464
GOOD NEIGHBOR PUBLICATIONS, INC.
21 N. LEMON ST., SARASOTA, FLORIDA
PRINTED IN THE UNITED STATES OF AMERICA

*A man thinks . . .*
*He thinks for himself . . .*
*He thinks positively.*
*This naturally leads to his belief in "doing justice, loving mercy and walking humbly at the side of God."*
*A man then translates belief into action.*

*This book is dedicated to two women . . .*

*My mother,* may her soul rest in peace, who showered me with affection, love and understanding. She gave me the spiritual foundation on which my life has been developed.

*My wife, Celia,* who is companion, sweetheart and friend. She put her faith in me, and gave me the inspiration and courage to complete this labor of love . . . my life story.

## *FOREWORD*

November 24, 1859 represents one of the most important dates in history. That day Charles Darwin gave to the world his "Origin of the Species by Means of Natural Selection"—more often referred to as the Theory of Evolution.

A great disciple of his put it this way: "Thus the ascent of man stood out very clearly. Man and ape were second cousins, born of a common stock and one could trace an imperceptible progression from the common ancestor, a primitive ape to modern man."

That was the time for educators, philosophers and psychologists to teach that the most important fact in the lives of human beings was to live spiritually in order to get as far removed from their animal cousins as possible.

They should have emphasized that to eat, drink, sleep, work, play and fornicate was not too different from what monkeys do. Schools should have started then to teach the child in the first grade that to hate another human being was to lower oneself to the level of a monkey. Our education should have had as its overwhelming objective the teaching of hate as being the single most important reason why wars come into being.

Since President Kennedy's assassination there have been thousands of articles written in every area of the globe plainly saying that hate is the prime cause of mankind's ills.

How much longer are we going to advance materially and stand still or retrogress spiritually? Haven't we given the home and church several thousand years to do the job? If only educators had realized one hundred years ago what is so apparent to all today, they would have seized the opportunity to prevent the World Wars. Surely that would be true of World War II, brought about by the greatest monkey of our time, Adolf Hitler. Had children in the schools been taught that hate is to the soul what cancer is to the body no one like Hitler could have risen to set the world on fire. He would have been ridiculed and laughed out of existence.

I confess to you that I have an obsession. It is that hate is the most destructive force in the world. Hate is for monkeys, but a luxury men cannot afford. I hope to have it come about that anyone known to hate another human being be referred to as a monkey.

That is why I have written this book. I am a man with average intelligence. I flunked out of two universities and never obtained a degree. Other than dress manufacturing I have no claim to fame. For over twenty years I have played golf and have never broken one hundred: I have played bridge over thirty years and among those who know I am considered a weak player. In over thirty-five years I have consistently lost money in investments of all kinds. I am ignorant of bird, animal and plant life. I know nothing about music.

Yet an ordinary fellow like myself has come into possession of the most profound truths because of love for God, lust for learning and the desire to grow as a man.

It hasn't been easy. It has taken a lifetime for me to develop into a person I can respect. It is my belief that you will not only enjoy reading this book, but that you will find something herein to stimulate your mind and help you grow.

That is what I hoped for in writing the story of my life. . . . How From a Monkey I Became a Man.

# CONTENTS

# HOW FROM A MONKEY I BECAME A MAN

## *From Tyranny to Liberty*

A log cabin is luxurious compared to the hovel where my four sisters, two brothers and I were born. My mother described it as a one-room structure with the bare earth as its floor, and a straw-thatched roof overhead. A large oven, almost the size of a baker's, covered one full side of the room. Several feet above the oven was a sort of balcony which served as sleeping quarters for all seven children, Sophie, Lottie, Tillie, Morris, Abe, Freda, and myself. Seven sleeping on one berth above the hot oven enabled us to keep warm in the cold winters. As for the summers, you can use your imagination.

This was in Russia where Napoleon and Hitler discovered how mean and treacherous the winters can be. It was in the village of Linkowitz in the State of Vohlynia where my story begins. The total population was under three hundred and we were one of the five Jewish families. Child mortality ran very high because of total lack of hygiene. Brushing one's teeth was not a practice of the villagers. We virtually lived in mud and filth just like the pigs in their sty. Life was rugged, indeed. The nearest doctor was twenty-four miles away and it took hours for him to come on the rare occasions he was called. The nearest midwife, and only midwives were used for obstetric purposes, was eight miles away. The weather was so bad when my brother Abe was born that my father could no longer bear to see my mother suffer in her labor. So, calling upon his Talmudic knowledge, he cleansed his hands, dipped them in oil and severed the cord that delivered a healthy bouncing boy.

It was strictly an agricultural community. My father did some farming, but chiefly he acted as agent for the villagers in trading their wheat and cattle in the nearby larger towns.

We lived in ignorance. We knew nothing of what went on in the world of commerce, politics, art, science or literature . . . magazines or even newspapers were unknown in the lives of the Linkowitzers. From early sun-up until long after sundown they toiled unceasingly. Their sweat could not even earn white bread. Black bread was the staff of life. Only during Easter did some peasants have the luxury of white bread.

On Sunday they attended the village Greek Catholic services. The Jewish families carried on their services without benefit of rabbi or cantor. For the Jewish Holidays the Jews of Tcherbok, four and a half miles away numbering six families, would get together with our five families.

Despite the pogroms that ravished the Jews in Russia, anti-semitism was unknown in our village. The Christians and Jews lived as one community. They celebrated one another's births, marriages and deaths. They laughed together and cried together.

In 1903 when I, the youngest, was but six months old, my father left for America. He wrote that he was fortunate in reaching St. Louis, Missouri, where friends prevailed upon him to give their children Hebrew lessons. This afforded him a meager livelihood, but he could not scrape together enough even at the end of a year, to send transportation to Sophie and Lottie, my two oldest sisters. With a loan from friends he did manage to bring them over in 1904. They both started working in the garment sweatshops for about $9.00 a week for sixty hours work. Through skimping and saving, they saved enough to send for Mother and the remaining five children in 1905.

For some reason Russia was not permitting her Jews to emigrate in that year. Our transportation tickets, therefore, could start only at a point in Galicia across the Russian boundaries. So, with the barest of means, we left Linkowitz, Russia, in the year 1905 for that Golden, Promised Land, the United States of America.

My mother was thirty-seven. Tillie, the third oldest, was sixteen, Morris, fourteen, Abe, eight, Freda, four and I just two and a half. A friend of ours, a peasant from the village, hitched up his team of horses, and took all our possessions and the six of us on the first lap of that long, long trek to America. He took us to Shepetovka, the nearest town where there was a railroad. Our destination was the last village on the Russian-Galician border, opposite the town of Radzivill. There it became our unpleasant and dangerous job to steal across the border in the still of the night.

That Friday night Mother lit her Sabbath candles in a stable in the very midst of the horses and their neighing. About midnight, four Galicians, whom my mother had bribed after learning from other Jews of their reliability, came to the stable to fetch us and our belongings. They wore rubber boots all the way up to their hips. They provided rubber boots for Mother and the children, excepting Freda and myself, who had to ride piggy-back on the shoulders of two of the men.

Obviously we could not steal across the border on dry land. They had to locate uninhabited marsh lands. A good deal of the time they had to wade through water three and four feet deep. This hike, but a few miles, took almost the whole night, because of the many difficulties. Always they had to fear the border patrolmen, who took pot shots into the marshes if they heard suspicious noises. Then there was little Abe, who had the toughest time of it between getting stuck in the mud and almost drowning. One can imagine that it was not the easiest matter to walk in rubber boots that weren't the right size, which stuck to the deep mud with almost every step. The psychological pressure of a mother with five children fleeing through marshland, with the necessity for arriving in a strange land before daybreak, was a "heroic legend" in itself.

With the aid of God and the untiring four "border leggers," dawn found us safe and sound at a tiny Galician village. We were given shelter for the Sabbath by fellow Jews. There was no place in the village for us to sleep, so we had to leave that very night. We hired a villager who took us in his wagon to the town of Brody. There we could use the transportation tickets to America.

Unfortunately, little Abe became ill from his ordeal, and we remained in Brody for two weeks. This almost exhausted the funds Mother had, so that it was a day of great rejoicing when we wearily boarded the train which was to cut across the heart of all Europe and bring us to Rotterdam. It was a four-day and three-night ride. We were not in a drawing room, pullman, or even a chair car. We rode in a cattle car all the way.

We arrived in Rotterdam without any money. The Jewish Relief Society cabled father at St. Louis and it took nine days before we received sufficient money to engage passage on a small freighter to Liverpool, England. Tillie and Morris stole fruit from the ship's cargo to keep us from starving. Perhaps it was punishment for their "crime" that all our baggage was lost or stolen on the freighter, so that we arrived in Liverpool without any clothes or belongings. Again a cable had to be sent to America and again we had to be recipients of aid from a

Jewish relief society in the ten days that we waited for a ship to take us across the Atlantic.

It was a good ship, the Republic, which sailed from Liverpool to Boston. It took nine days and we were put in steerage. The trip could not have been a pleasant one.

Mother, being highly emotional and taxed to the limit of her endurance, literally fell on her knees and kissed the cold earth of America as soon as we walked off the gangplank at the dock in Boston. The following day we were riding on an American train, seated as first class human beings en route to St. Louis, Missouri.

Imagine the scene at the Union Station in St. Louis, when the father who had not seen his wife and children for two years, when the oldest girls who hadn't seen the family for a year, greeted and embraced one another. Composed on-lookers must have considered us a noisy, uncouth bunch of foreigners. One wonders if any had the spirit of compassion to imagine what constituted the background of that noisy reception, where, amid the uncontained joy, many tears were shed.

We were taken to Eleventh Street near Biddle, the poorest section of the ghetto. Yet to us it was like a "little bit of Heaven." Compared to what we had left behind in Linkowitz, the cobbled stone streets and the three-room flat were wonderful indeed. Above all else, it was a family of seven children and their parents reunited under one roof, in the most wonderful country in the universe. What did it matter that nine of us lived in three small rooms? Wasn't it better than the one room, mud floor and straw roof to which we were accustomed?

ENTERPRISE AND EDUCATION

## *Folks Try Business—I Start to School*

Mother's enterprising nature could not approve of Papa as a Hebrew teacher and earning four dollars a week. Just what could a man of my father's background do in the U.S.A.? Farming? In the first place, where would we raise the money to buy a farm? In the second place, even if we could, why should we go back to the desolation and existence of living on a farm or village, once we had tasted the unlimited cultural possibilities which the city, even the ghetto, afforded? Especially were we appreciative of the privilege long denied us of going to the crowded synagogue on the Sabbath and Holy Days. There we met people and made friends.

After much consideration, it was decided that Papa should open a kosher meat market. This was a business rather than a profession, and that is where Mother thought he belonged; yet he could conduct it so that it did not interfere with our rigid orthodox observance of the Sabbath and Holy Days.

I remember the butcher shop on Ninth Street between Wash Street and Franklin Avenue. Next door, to the right, was the entrance to the "small Ninth Street synagogue"; next to that was the small Jewish bathhouse, and on the corner of Ninth and Washington streets was the big Ninth Street synagogue. Opposite the synagogue was the imposing Jefferson Public School. To the left of our store was Fisher's Grocery Store; then the hallway that led to the tenements above the stores, and in back of the stores. One was Jackman's, the other Lesser's and the third was Gottesman's. It seemed as if our block was a center for tailors' woolens and other supplies.

To be closer to the butcher shop we moved from Eleventh Street to Wash Street near Ninth. We were the only Jews living in the house tenanted by Italians and owned by the Rizzo's. In fact, Wash Street from Seventh to Eleventh was more Italian than Jewish. We got along wonderfully well with our Italian neighbors. They were a warm, generous, sentimental type who would, with broad smiles, invariably pinch my cheeks with genuine affection. As in Linkowitz, Russia, here too we went to their weddings, births and funerals and they attended ours, proving that good neighbors can exist anywhere. There was an especially strong feeling of attachment between the Rizzo and Goldfarb families.

I remember the preparation made for my entering kindergarten at the Jefferson School when I was five years old. One might have thought I was being sent away to a fancy boarding school. Since Mother was busy at the butcher shop, it fell to my sister Tillie to run the household.

Tillie went to Gordon's Dry Goods Store to get me some nice blouses and knickers. She bought me a cap and a few pairs of black ribbed stockings; a pair of shoes at Golman's on Morgan Street. The night before I started to school she gave me a good hot bath in the big wash tub into which she constantly added steaming water.

In the morning she dressed me like a Little Lord Fauntleroy and pasted down my unruly hair with Vaseline. I was now all slicked up, and taking me by the hand, Tillie led me across the street to make my grand entrance into the public school.

JEW CONSCIOUSNESS

## *A Dose of Anti-Semitism*

When I had been in kindergarten only a few days, the children started to call me "Cockeye." It was the first time I had been aware of the fact that my eyes were crossed. Never from that time until many years later, when they were straightened, was I ever unmindful of being cross-eyed. Soon I was inured to being called "Cockeye," but then I began to be called "Sheeny" by some Italian kids. I was to learn the venom and hate which the Roman Catholic Italian children bore the Jews. On Tenth and Wash there was a Roman Catholic Church. One day I passed there and three or four Italian boys jumped on me yelling "Sheeny." They frightened the life out of me as they grabbed me and forced me to get down on my knees and kiss a crucifix. Then they lectured to me about being a Christ Killer, pelted me a few times, and I felt lucky I could run back home alive.

It was the first time I had ever heard the name of Christ mentioned, so I asked Tillie what the children meant by referring to me as a Christ Killer and forcing me to kiss the cross. Tillie did her best to explain to me about the hatred of gentiles toward Jews. When I told her about the Rizzos, the Shtabudos, the Sansonis and other neighbors, she said, "Oh, that's different. They're our neighbors; they know and love us." In my simple, child's mind I wondered why a block should make such a difference—why the other Italians should fail to know and love us.

With the passing months my education in anti-Semitism increased markedly. Soon I became aware of continuous street brawls between Jewish and Italian boys, and between the Jews and the Irish of the adjacent neighborhood called the Kerry Patch district. Then one day when I was at the butcher shop I saw my father come back with his horse and delivery wagon. I noticed he was disheveled and distraught. I learned that the Kosher sign on the delivery wagon, and the fact that he wore a beard, marked him as a subject for attack in the Kerry Patch district. They threw stones at him, shattered the side windows of the wagon, and ordered him to stay out of their neighborhood. At another time my brother Morris came back from East St. Louis with black eyes and a bloody nose. I asked, "Italians?" He answered between sobs, "No, the dirty Poles." So I came to realize that anti-Semitism wasn't confined to one group of gentiles, but to all, insofar as I could comprehend. I overheard conversations later between my father and brother Morris that there were nice gentiles who would never bother the Jews. They referred especially to the "clean Germans" on the South Side. From then on I had a very soft spot in my heart for the German people.

Needless to say, we Jews, both adults and children, soon learned to know where the danger spots were and tried to avoid them. Nevertheless, my kind, gentle father was often the victim of hoodlum attacks. All of us were vulnerable to the war of nerves occasioned by the threat of the gentile hoodlums. It is easy to understand why semi-literate foreigners such as we were, developed hate and contempt for our persecutors and for the Catholic religion with which they were all associated. The sight of priests or nuns signified to us the "brains" who were instigating and directing these hoodlums by their false teaching of Jesus Christ's death. We were especially superstitious of nuns, and made it a habit to close our mouths tightly when they passed; otherwise, we felt they counted our teeth and they would fall out!

The freedom and economic security we enjoyed in

America was largely offset by constant anxiety, strain and utter terror.

COCKEYE FOR PRESIDENT

## *I Receive Charity*

When I was seven years old, and in the second grade, my class was asked to write on the subject of what we wanted to be when we grew up. Most children wrote they wanted to be cowboys, policemen and firemen. I wrote that I wanted to be President of the United States, so that I could make it impossible for one people to attack another because of their religion.

My teacher was very proud of me for writing that piece. She gave me a note to Mother stating how exceptional were the thoughts I expressed and telling her it was being put on the bulletin board near the principal's office.

Fortunately, for me, our calisthenics teacher, Mr. Nathan, read my piece on the bulletin board. He took an interest in me. He asked why I didn't wear glasses to correct my crossed-eyes. Then he gave me a letter to the Aloe Optical Company, which magically procured glasses for me. In a few years my eyes were in focus but the world I knew still appeared to be "cock-eyed."

NEGRO FRIENDS

## *I Learn Tolerance*

I spent a great deal of my time in the butcher shop. It was a long narrow store. A long high counter, about the height of a tavern bar, extended from the front window about thirty feet clear back to the big ice box. In front of the counter were high stools for the customers. The floor was generally covered with saw-dust. Alongside the one bare wall there was usually stacked a bunch of coops housing some ducks and geese, but mostly chickens. Water troughs were on each of the coops and corn was thrown into them for the fowl to feed upon. This job I soon took over.

Another job, however, took my fancy. In the rear of the store, behind the big ice box, was the place where the "Shochet" (authorized by Jewish law to slaughter animals and fowl) would slaughter the fowl.

He had a finished style of grabbing it, placing it between his legs, turning its head with his left hand; then, while holding the sharp knife between his teeth, he would use his right hand to pluck the fine feathers of the neck clear down to the skin. He would say a certain prayer in Hebrew, thanking God for the privilege of sanctifying the food; and then—swish—he would pull the knife across the throat forcing the blood to ooze out. He would drop the fowl to the floor, where often it would continue to struggle for a few minutes before it collapsed.

The fowl killed, it became the job of the pluckers to remove the feathers. For that purpose we had a colored couple whose names were Charlie and Emma. Sometimes when we were especially busy, such as before the Holy

Days, they would bring another man to help them. His name was Henry. We never established whether Charlie and Emma were legally married but they lived together in the back of the store for all the years we were in business there.

Charlie was very tall and skinny. I never saw him without a hat or bonnet of some kind. His mustache always showed white streaks from the duck feathers that clung to it. He was an ugly-looking specimen but as kindly a soul as I have ever known. Emma was short and wiry and gave off an odor worse than Charlie, since they hardly ever took a bath.

Henry was short and fat. He had a Van Dyke beard which naturally attracted the feathers. He had a peg leg which he exposed from the knee down. He was far more dignified than either Charlie or Emma. He spoke very little. Charlie did some talking, but Emma—she talked without ever stopping to catch her breath.

Every chance I got I would sit down, as they did, on an apple box and grab a fowl and start plucking. I would join them in song and in conversation when Emma permitted anyone to speak. About every hour or so they would get up, all three of them, and go around the corner to a saloon that was known as "905," simply because that was the address on Franklin Avenue where it was located.

I never remember a time when any of the trio were without a few drinks under their belts, yet the occasion was rare when Henry or Charlie got drunk. Now with Emma it was a different story. Often she came back from one of her trips to "905" in a nasty, boisterous mood. She would come into the room where they worked, from the rear entrance, and if she spotted me, her greeting to me would usually be "You no good Christ Killer, son-of-a-bitch, I'se gwine to kill you, sho' nuff!" I had long ago gotten over being afraid of her threats, though on one occasion she ran into the butcher shop, picked up a meat cleaver, and chased me for blocks.

You could hardly blame her when I tell you what infuriated her. In one of her sullen, sulking moods instead of cussin' and hollerin', she was mumbling to herself. Just like a buzz saw, she kept chatting to herself while plucking away. She was so drunk it was surprising she could remain awake. Then an inspiration came to me. First I filled a can with water, and getting behind her, I lightly sprinkled her kinky hair. She was aware that drops of water were dropping on her but she treated the situation as if she were sitting under a light rainfall. Then I took a basketful of the soft down feathers, plucked from freshly slaughtered ducks, and gently covered her entire head.

Charlie and Henry were laughing their fool heads off. "What you all laughin' for, you coal-black niggers?" Emma repeated over and over again. Finally, Henry walked over to her, grabbed her by the arm and took her to the big mirror at the front of the big ice box. That's when she "saw red" and picked up the cleaver and came after me. For many days afterward I kept out of Emma's sight.

On the whole, however, our relationship with Charlie, Emma and Henry was one of mutual respect. We respected them for the genuine affection they bore our entire family, for their loyalty and devotion. They respected us because they knew my folks understood them and did not patronize them. By word and deed, Mother and Dad conveyed the fact to them that only by the grace of God are we born, whatever we are born.

## *Punishment to Fit the Crime*

I was about eight and a half years old the day I found a dollar bill at my mother's bedside. I immediately went to my sister Freda and together we laid plans for disposing of it. We went to the candy store and bought many pennies' worth of candy, as against our usual expenditure of only a cent at a time. Freda bought a five-cent imitation doll and I bought a five-cent ball. Then we bought a ten-cent tin bank and put the balance of our coins into it. It was a field day for Freda and me, and a good thing, too, that I was unaware of the fact that Freda had "spilled the beans" and told Mother. Instead, however, of telling the whole truth and of her collaboration in the matter, Freda said, "Sammy stole a dollar and spent it at the candy store." At least it was a great day, even if I was to experience the greatest surprise that night.

After we had our dinner, I noticed we were being visited by my three married sisters and their husbands. I could not understand what prompted this mid-week visit. It wasn't long, however, before I discovered the reason. Father asked us all to come into the living room and be seated. Then he solemnly proceeded to say that he had sent Abe as a messenger to fetch them so that they would be present to witness the punishment one member of the family was to receive because of thievery. He then asked for me to come toward him. He removed the strap from the trousers he was wearing. I did not appreciate the significance of his action because I had never in my life received corporal punishment from my parents. "You have broken the Commandment "Thou shalt not steal," my father went on to admonish me. "Though you have committed many improper acts I have never punished you, for I charged it to childish behavior. When, however, you break any of the Ten Commandments, I feel it my duty to God to punish you." He placed me across his knee and beat my backside with the strap; and he wasn't fooling. He was so zealous in representing the Lord that he might never have stopped because of my crying and yelling. Only when Mother intervened did he release me. I lay on the floor with my face down, sobbing. I could not for a single moment glance up into the faces of the whole family, who now knew me to be a thief, a breaker of the Commandments. Humiliation and shame were my lot.

My sister Tillie soon came to me and used all her strength to raise me from the floor where I was intent on spending the whole night. She said that Father was right and had to punish me to prevent my doing future wrongs. When I managed to blurt out that Freda was "my partner in crime" Tillie ran to tell the family about it. Then they all gathered around me. It was decided that since Freda had acted with me, and since we had put most of the money in the bank, it was not to be considered thievery.

MISTER PIAN IS KILLED

## *A Glimpse of Tragedy*

At this time, I was to become acquainted with tragedy in the ghetto. First came the great shock of hearing of the suicide of my friend Sidney Gottesman's father. It created much speculation among all the neighbors since no one could discover the reason for his doing away with himself. He was not known to be ill. His business was in good shape and his domestic life was considered ideal.

A few weeks later, while playing in the back alley of Franklin Avenue, we heard men shouting and we saw a gang chasing a Negro on Tenth Street. We rushed to the street and learned that Mr. Sam Pian, proprietor of the jewelry store on the corner of Tenth and Franklin had been shot by the Negro. Along with the other boys, I forced my way into the jewelry store and managed to get a glimpse of the dead body lying in the center of the floor. The police had not yet arrived, but a clerk was excitedly telling some onlooker what had happened. It was not a hold-up. The murder took place because of an argument over payment of installments which the Negro owed the jeweler.

I walked away downcast. I had seen the change that being fatherless had wrought in the lives of the Gottesman children. Now I kept thinking that the same would happen to the Pian children.

FEAST, THEN FUNERAL

## *Papa Rejoices; Papa Dies*

It was my ninth birthday and my brother Morris' engagement to Lena Tofield, a beautiful and charming girl from New York. It was the occasion for a triple celebration, for I had just learned to translate the first book of the Bible from the Hebrew into Yiddish. I never recall my father in a more jubilant mood than that Sunday when the entire family and friends gathered to attend the party. About seventy-five people crowded into our dingy three-room flat. The three married sisters spent all of that morning and early afternoon turning the place upside down to make it clean and as cheerful as possible.

Long table-tops were set up on wooden horses in the

living room. White table cloths, extra special size, were borrowed for the occasion. All the neighbors chipped in to lend us silverware, dishes, cooking utensils, glassware and a variety of chairs.

The tables when set were a feast for the eyes. Pains were taken to arrange the luscious fruit in huge bowls at alternating positions on the table, to be most decorative and appealing. The egg glossy surface of the extra large loaves of twisted bread cause me even now to smack my lips thinking about them. This was all in readiness before any of the guests were seated.

Naturally there wasn't enough room for all to be seated and served. Only about half the company could join the immediate family at the tables. The others were served "buffet" in the kitchen and bedroom and a few on the back porch. I am sure the latter were not offended as it was the custom at such parties to give priority in seating and service to the nearest of kin, while the more distant relatives and friends cheerfully resigned themselves to second class treatment.

I was as proud as a peacock after the last dinner course because, before saying grace, Father apprised the guests of my progress in my Hebrew studies. He asked all to raise their glasses for a toast which was to the effect that I should always prize learning above earning, and that I was always to be a good Jew, a credit to Israel.

That was the happiest moment I had ever spent in the presence of my father. Otherwise I saw very little of him, since he arose at four o'clock in the morning and went to sleep right after his dinner. I never remember much contact with Dad. He always impressed me as stern and puritanical in his make-up. I had heard my sisters tell of his extraordinary will power and devotion to our religion. For instance, he had given up eating those dishes which he considered delicacies or extra-appetizing. He loved chicken livers, but refused to eat them because he believed one should forego many choice and desirable things to discipline one's will power.

On Saturdays and Holy Days, Brother Abe and I accompanied Dad to synagogue, but few words were ever exchanged between us. Solemnly we would march along with him and take our places at the East wall. At times in the service the priests chant a certain prayer which requires the congregation to cover their eyes. Then my father would raise his very large prayer shawl and cuddle both Abe and me near him while the three of us remained covered by the shawl until the few minutes of the service expired. It gave me much satisfaction to get so close to my father, who otherwise was not demonstrative or affectionate as was my mother.

Only a few months after my birthday party the greatest tragedy struck me. My father died after a short siege of pneumonia. I was told he had never before been ill a day in his life. Looking back, I wonder that a man in such humble circumstances could have had so large an attendance at his funeral. It seemed to me that the carriages and horses were lined up for several blocks.

At the grave it took several strong men to restrain my mother from her attempts to throw herself into it, when the grave diggers began to cover the coffin with earth.

My parents had been married twenty-eight years. They quarreled much because Mother was my father's superior intellectually, culturally and especially in business. She bluntly tried to dominate by sheer virtue of her superiority instead of exercising patience and psychology to get her way. Yet they loved each other dearly.

Family picture 1908: (*standing*) Lottie, Morris, Tillie, Sophie. (*Middle row*) Frank Hoffman, Father, Freda, Mother, Sam Sherman. (*Front row*) Abe and author.

Sister Tillie, brother Morri
and niece Florence. Autho
holding niece Evelyn wa
16 but only the size of a 1
year old.

Eli (*left*), the author's partner in crime. Sammy (*standing*), age 14, when he stole to
play stud poker and shoot
pool for $5 a game in Gales-
burg, Ill.

With Mother, Abe and Freda. After Papa's death, in the year of mourning (1912), Mother laid the spiritual foundation on which he built his life.

MOURNING WITH MOTHER

## *The Most Unforgettable Character I Ever Knew*

Mother had all the qualities that a widow without money, at forty-five years of age, could possibly have. She was truly beautiful. She was dynamic, learned, cultured and above all the essence of spirituality. The marriage brokers were hot on her trail after the year's mourning period was over. I remember that for years afterward countless suitors sought her hand in marriage. She, however, did not give them the slightest consideration. Thirty-four years passed after Father died but Mother remained faithful to his love and passed up all chances for companionship that the many marriage offers held.

Father left barely enough to cover funeral expenses. Mother tried to operate the butcher shop with the aid of my thirteen-year-old brother and eleven-year-old sister and myself. Three older sisters and one brother were married. The three of us would get up at five-thirty in the morning. First we boys went to synagogue to say the Kaddish prayers which Orthodox Jews recite during the first year of mourning. Next we helped ourselves to a makeshift breakfast prepared on the kitchen coal stove. We had no gas or electricity in the three-room apartment over the butcher shop. In fact, we had to get our water from a pipe on the porch and we used the out-house in the backyard, which we shared with thirty other tenement neighbors. Then we would trot down to the shop where Mother had been working since four o'clock when the packing houses made their deliveries. She had laid out several quarters of beef and with saw and cleaver trimmed and cut out the orders, which we three would deliver to our "swell customers" in the west end of town. Leaving the ghetto about seven o'clock, each of us had two baskets to lug on the noisy trolley cars, which usually made me car sick. The big idea was to manipulate a five cent ride to cover most of our route on one fare. This was possible through the generous transfer system which enabled us to go from one line to another.

My route was in the area surrounding Washington University. Somehow it never aroused envy in my heart when I appraised the beauty, warmth and spaciousness of the homes I entered. I simply took it for granted that certain people were born to live well, and others to struggle as we did. I did, however, conjure up in my mind the vision of some day being a student at the University. This dream I dreamt every time the trolley passed its magnificent grounds.

About eight-forty we returned from our deliveries just in time to hear the school bell. Then I envied the children who, though poor like ourselves, had the opportunity to play in the school yard for half an hour or so before the bell summoned us indoors.

In the year that we mourned my father's death, we children were not permitted to indulge in any entertainment such as going to the Nickelodeon, listening to the phonograph or any music. It was a solemn year, indeed.

It was, however, fun when we went to the public bath house Friday afternoons to be clean for synagogue service and to usher in the Sabbath eve. Mother and Sis sat in the balcony, where the women prayed. Abe and I felt quite manly being on our own among the men of the synagogue, and especially so at the end of services. Then the congregation was completely hushed while Abe's alto and my soprano voice joined in unison to say "Yis gadal, v'yiskadash" the traditional Hebrew prayer said every day during the year of mourning for the departed and thereafter on the anniversaries of their deaths. We could hear Mother crying in the balcony all the time we were standing and chanting the prayer. After services, brother Abe asked the sexton whether some poor stranger was in the congregation, so we could bring him home to share our Sabbath eve dinner.

Sabbath Day services started at eight in the morning and were over about noon. After lunch Mother ushered us into our bleak living room, which was the only room with windows. While she sat on the rocker, Abe, Sis and I sat on the floor. Then for about two hours Mother read aloud stories from the Bible. Mother was a great storyteller. She had a way of holding our interest and transmitting to us the moral of each story. Mother was obsessed with the idea that giving is living. Over and over again she preached to us that all our material aspirations should be for the sole purpose of being better able to give to the less fortunate.

About three o'clock in the afternoon on Sabbath days, Mother's story sessions would end. She would retire for a much-needed nap. Sis would go out to play while Abe and I went back to the synagogue. There the learned of the congregation were seated along both sides of a long table while the others stood around and listened, to pick up bits of Talmudic wisdom. We, of course, were among the standees. About four-thirty o'clock there was a buffet repast, the main dish being marinated herring or gefilte fish, which the women of the congregation took turns in supplying. Then after grace was said and for half an hour before late afternoon services commenced, there was group singing which, as mourners, Abe and I could not join. We, nevertheless, enjoyed witnessing the turn from a day of solemn prayer and meditation to one of mirth and joy. It was good to see those anemic-looking, bearded

Jews throw off the burdens and cares of the entire week and enter into a spirit of gaiety.

Late afternoon services were followed by evening services. That marked the end of the Sabbath, yet one additional service remained: the ushering in of the new week. The congregation would stand around the prayer reader who was giving thanks to God for the privilege of entering into a week of service. The highlight of the service occurred when the reader lit a little alcohol spilled on a saucer. This created a huge flame, which all members standing around would eagerly and joyously grasp with their fingers. Then we all ran our own fingers quickly across our eyes, ears and forehead. The holy flame was to consecrate us to a life of service for the forthcoming week.

Mother heroically carried on the heavy work of a butcher. Everyone in the neighborhood and all the customers admired and respected her. They indulged her as they would no other butcher. At the busiest hour near noon, even when a dozen or so customers were at the counter, she would hurriedly remove the blood-stained white butcher's apron and run like mad to the school where it was recess time, and the children were at play. With her she carried two packages of something; pears with bread and butter, cookies, or anything else she knew we liked. First she went to the girls' playground on Ninth Street and found Freda waiting behind the iron fence to receive her package. Then, continuing at a mad pace, she turned around the corner to Wash Street where the boys' playground was located. Here Abe and I were on the receiving end. She always kissed us as she gave us the goodies which we relished so much. I can't remember if any other children's parents engaged in this daily practice. When the circumstances are considered it reveals the love and sacrifice of our mother.

Her goodness knew no bounds. Though carrying on a business few men could operate without help, she found the time, God only knows how, to bake cakes for the various synagogue affairs. She might have been the inspiration for the one who coined the expression "He'd give the shirt off his back." On several occasions after a Saturday afternoon visit she returned home with her coat tightly around her but without any dress underneath. We had gotten over being surprised about such actions because we already knew Mother would give her dress to some other poor woman pointed out by a friend. She was a "sucker" for any touch. Every waking moment she was obsessed by the need of giving, sharing, taking care of the less fortunate.

Though she had little to give, she gave it all, and most graciously. There was no such thing as "you can't give to everything" in her thinking. "Why not?" she would counter, "If you can't give tens you can give dollars; if you can't give dollars, you give dimes, and if need be, pennies; but by all means, give to every worthy cause."

In honesty and humility I can truthfully say I have, in a lifetime of association with philanthropy, never seen such a "giver" as was my mother. She constantly reminded us that even more important than giving was to get others to give. It was selfish, she reasoned, to enjoy the blessings of giving without persuading others to share that blessing.

## *A Lesson I Shall Never Forget*

When school let out at three-thirty, my brother Abe, sister Freda and I would go across the street to the Hebrew school conducted by my mother's brother. When we got there, Uncle Harry would invariably be holding a glass of tea in his left hand and be nibbling sugar from a piece he had in his right hand. The Russian samovar was forever being tapped by him, for it seemed as if he were a chain tea drinker. I can't remember the time when during school hours Uncle Harry wasn't drinking tea except when expostulating on the subject matter of the moment.

I was then able to translate the first two books of the Bible from Hebrew to Yiddish. It was considered just a fair accomplishment for the nephew of an instructor who was bent on training me to become a rabbi. For every mistake I made, and they were numerous, Uncle Harry would take the middle and index fingers of his right hand and grab the highest part of my cheek. Then he would twist his finger from left to right clockwise. Usually this action was accompanied by some remark in Yiddish such as "If I didn't have such high aspirations for your future, I wouldn't punish you so severely."

I hated Uncle Harry and his school, but I loved his wife, my wonderful Aunt Sarah.

She was as sweet and soft as he was sour and gruff. It seemed to me as if she never let the heels of her shoes touch the ground. She walked as on tip-toe all the time. I can't remember when Aunt Sarah wasn't smiling. When she slyly slipped me a poppy seed cookie of her own baking and I saw her angelic smile, it took the sting out of the burning cheek Uncle Harry had just inflicted on me.

Most women in the ghetto walked with bowed heads and hunched shoulders, most often with knitted brows on faces exposed from shawls that covered their bodies to below their hips. Aunt Sarah walked erectly and the serene expression on her face conveyed the impression that she had just been the recipient of good news.

I wondered how she could be so happy with a sourpuss like Uncle Harry. They were childless, but I never knew that they had had any children, until one day I overheard the mother of one of my classmates speaking to Aunt Sarah in the kitchen. "Tell me, Sarah, what is it that keeps you so cheerful and understanding while most of us grumble and complain? I know you are so strong of character that I can speak of the fact that you had two sons who died before their teens. None of us have experienced such sorrow, yet we dwell upon our poverty and sickness. What is the secret of your balance, your patience, your consideration for others?"

I heard Aunt Sarah's answer, "My dear Mrs. Gottesman, I find it so simple, so natural to behave as I do. I cannot comprehend how one can act differently if one has deep convictions about one's faith. The trouble with most people comes from the fact that they don't have their faith deeply rooted, so that the slightest crisis frustrates them.

"Now I genuinely believe in the God of our Bible. I believe He created us and it is for Him alone to determine our destiny. Who are we to challenge the ways of the Lord? Didn't Hannah of old lose her eight sons? Yet faith in God sustained her and she said, 'God giveth and God taketh.' Now, instead of constantly mourning the loss of my children, I rejoice at the memories of the times I spent with them. Moreover, I would not want their spirits to discover me to be unfaithful to all I taught them. God demands of us that we go on living and loving all the days of our life on earth. We cannot serve God or man well by being frustrated and unhappy."

Never in the fifty-three years that have passed have I been able to eradicate the memory of that conversation between Mrs. Gottesman and my aunt Sarah.

I had not seen Aunt Sarah since Uncle Harry died, about ten years after Father's death. Uncle Harry had moved his Hebrew School to a better section of the ghetto and prospered sufficiently to leave a $6,000.00 house, unencumbered, as a legacy to his widow. In his will he stipulated that when Aunt Sarah died the proceeds from the sale of the house were to be divided equally between her next of kin and his sister Sarah who was then even worse off than my mother, who now had grown children to support her. Well, what do you suppose Aunt Sarah did? She immediately sold the house for $6,000.00 and gave $3,000.00 to her husband's sister with these words: "Here, Sarah, is the $3,000.00 my husband wanted you to have upon my death. I figured I would give it to you now so that instead of patiently waiting for me to die you would joyously pray for me to live!"

Soon after her year of mourning she married a fine rabbi from Philadelphia and both of them went to Palestine, where they lived out their lives.

SHARES HIS BREAD WITH OTHERS

## *Laborer on Strike*

About a year and a half after Father died, Mother sold the store, and was left with about three hundred dollars. Sophie urged us to come to Galesburg to live with her. Abe, now sixteen, could work for her husband who operated a shoe store. Mother sent Abe and Freda to Galesburg, Illinois, but took me with her to Chicago.

She could not have picked a more inopportune time to park us with sister Lottie. For at that very time my brother-in-law was one of the many thousand garment workers on strike. We soon learned their circumstances. They were receiving under three dollars a week as strike benefits from the union. They were being carried "on the cuff" by the grocer and butcher and were knee-deep in debt. Their situation was desperate, but slightly ameliorated by the fact that Frank's nephew, a poor farmer, sent them a whole sack of potatoes and onions.

Less than three dollars a week income for a family of four had to be stretched to take care of six. If you think it less than morale-breaking, play a game trying to figure twelve dollars a month for rent, fuel for the stoves, food, shoes and clothing with only fourteen dollars monthly income. Yet in such a crisis I once eavesdropped at bedtime and overheard Lottie speaking to Frank. "We'll have to ask them to go," referring to Mother and me.

Then crude, semi-literate Frank rose to majestic heights on the ladder of morality when, without a moment's consideration, he replied, "Positively not. They will stay here until we are put out on the streets. As long as we have a loaf of bread, they will share a third of it."

And stay we did, for several months, until the strike was settled.

GALESBURG

## *My First Paid Job*

Mother and I missed Freda and Abe, so we eventually moved to Galesburg, Illinois, to settle down with Sophie. Fortunately, the Shermans had a lovely, airy six-room flat and made good use of every inch of space. In addition to Mother and her three children, my brother-in-law's mother and two of her younger sons, Charlie and Eli, were to share the one home. There wasn't a housing shortage then, but necessity born of poverty, forced three families of nine persons to live together. And we lived happily! Abe paired off with Charlie, who was about the same age, while Eli was only a few months older than I. Soon, however, Charlie moved to Aurora, Illinois, to work for his brother Dave. That made a little more room around the dinner table. Coming from the crowded ghetto of St. Louis and a slightly better one in Chicago, I found Galesburg a heavenly place in which to live.

My brother-in-law struggled to make a living in his store at 43 Seminary Street. Abe was his main clerk, but Eli and I at twelve years of age pitched in by working after school from three-thirty to ten at night (when the store closed) and all day Saturday, from eight-thirty A.M. to eleven P.M. Abe got $2.50 a week for at least eighty hours work. Eli and I were paid twenty-five cents to start and graduated to one dollar at the end of the year, for about fifty hours work each week. Of course, we all got our board and felt we were contributing to the support of our mothers.

It was a long, tedious grind. I hated Saturdays, for when we were the busiest, working hardest and tied down to almost midnight, the town was at its liveliest and almost all its citizens appeared to be celebrating. I envied the customers who came in all "spruced up" to make the most of the big night. About seventy-five per cent of the people were railroaders, the balance mostly farmers. On week days we seldom saw the farmers, but the railroad workers would run in often, especially after we had added men's furnishings.

During the week I remember them always in their overalls and typical caps and gloves. I suppose they must have lost gloves often, for it seemed as if they were forever buying them. Some bought the plain white canvas, while others preferred leather palms in either the wrist or gauntlet types. Most of our customers were brakemen, switchmen or those who worked in the shops of the Chicago, Burlington and Quincy Railroad. Here and there we had a few firemen and engineers from both the C.B. and Q. and the Atchison, Topeka and Santa Fe. We had very few conductors. The latter group, representing the higher paid railroad workers, seldom shopped on Seminary, which was a side-street shopping center. They went to Main Street, a few shopping at Stamm's, Bernstin and Penney's, but most of them going to the aristocrat of merchants, Jacobi Brothers and Mack and the O. T. Johnson Department Store. We spoke with bated breath when we referred to engineers and conductors, and we measured our every word and act when waiting on them. Even on weekdays we would never find the faces of the engineers or conductors smudged with grease or oil, but we would be surprised if switchmen, firemen, or brakemen entered the store with clean faces.

Saturday was different. You couldn't tell a switchman from an engineer, or a brakeman from a conductor unless you knew them personally, for all came in to the store dressed in their holiday best.

Eli and I would bemoan our fate. Whenever would the time come that we too could take part in the gaiety and excitement of Saturday night?

Sundays were blue days because Galesburg had what is known as the Blue Sunday laws, which meant all places of amusement were closed. Half the time we sat around moping because we could not go to the movies. Sometimes we visited the Michelsons, who had a houseful of youngsters—Harry, Bessie, Hannah, Hankee, Libby and Mickey—all ages and sizes. From the first time I saw her, I had a crush on Hannah and made it a point to play with her at every opportunity.

Occasionally Eli and I would walk along the railroad tracks, jumping from tie to tie until we were good and tired. We always enjoyed exploring the beautiful grounds of the small but famous Knox College. On one of the trees a tablet revealed the fact that at that spot one of the celebrated Lincoln-Douglas debates took place.

Sunday nights were usually spent by the entire family listening to fine music on the phonograph. The one luxury my brother-in-law indulged in was buying those expensive Red Seal recordings of the most famous opera stars. Caruso and Galli-Curci were our favorites.

DES MOINES

## *We Are Exposed to Democracy*

Mother became restless sitting around with little to do except help Sophie with the housework. So after considerable correspondence with Tillie, it was decided that she take Freda and me to Des Moines where Mother was to open the first Jewish delicatessen. I finished the seventh grade in the Galesburg elementary school. I was eleven when I entered the eighth grade of Crocker School in Des Moines, Iowa. Freda had been absent from school so much of the time because of illness, it gave me the opportunity to catch up to her, so that from then on to our graduation from high school in 1919, we were always in the same grade.

In Des Moines we moved into my sister Tillie's pleasant four-room flat on Third Street. It was many months before Mother found a location to open a delicatessen store. In the meantime, my brother-in-law's eighteen dollars a week salary had to be stretched to take care of three additional boarders. Never did I hear a word of complaint or grumbling from Tillie or Sam. On the contrary, they made it evident that we were wanted and did everything to make us happy. Sam taught me how to play checkers and we would play for hours in the evenings.

Finally, Mother took the plunge and opened a small delicatessen shop in the old Savery Hotel Building at Fourth and Locust streets. It was the first time the word Kosher spelled out in Hebrew letters ever appeared on any store on the west side of Des Moines. The few Kosher markets were all in the less populated section known as East Des Moines. The store was no howling success, but it made a living for us. At any rate, it took a load off the Ludmeyers who, God bless them, had made a real sacrifice to house the widowed mother-in-law and the orphans.

There was a Conservative Synagogue on Third Street where Rabbi Herman Cohen was then officiating. There I was being groomed for my Bar Mitzvah ceremony. This is the custom for Jewish boys at the age of thirteen, but is performed at the age of twelve in the case of boys without fathers. The Bar Mitzvah ceremony signifies that a boy is taking his place among the men of the house of Israel. So to alleviate the burdens of widowhood, the orphan son was therefore permitted entry into manhood a year earlier. In this case the boy generally assumed responsibilities sooner and was of help to his mother.

Those were happy days in the Crocker School until three o'clock and at the Third Street Hebrew School from three-thirty to five-thirty. At the latter I was initiated into the modern Hebrew School, altogether unlike the "face-slapping" one my uncle operated. If unruly, the boys were sent home and the parents were notified. My classmates were wonderful boys. I never got over thinking how nice these Des Moines children were to permit me, a poor widow's son, to be on a par with them in every respect. They invited me into their homes and introduced me to all members of their families. I shall always feel grateful to those fellows for giving me a lesson in democracy. They made me feel that I "belonged."

My family was proud of the way in which I carried out the duties on my Bar Mitzvah Sabbath. It was Saturday, nearest the eighteenth day of December in 1914. I read my portion from the Torah (scroll containing the five books of Moses) in a way that indicated I had received a thorough Hebrew education. My mother was very happy when Rabbi Cohen assured her after the service that none of his pupils had ever excelled my recitation.

Though I had received my Hebrew training and had my Bar Mitzvah ceremony at the Third Street Synagogue on the west side, Mother wouldn't think of worshipping there on the High Holy Days of the New Year and Yom Kippur (Day of Atonement.) Then she had to go to the most orthodox synagogue in town, which was called the Second Street Shule and was in East Des Moines where Rabbi Zeitchik officiated. He was a grand old gentleman, who at this writing is the Rabbi Emeritus of that same synagogue.

I was a choir boy who sang with the Cantor and some half dozen other youngsters. I sang most of the solos, a source of endless delight to Mother. She often repeated the statement that neighboring ladies in the balcony made, to the effect that "blessed was the womb that brought such a learned and talented child into the world."

In February 1916 Freda and I were graduated from grammar school. At graduation, when we were called upon to receive our diplomas, it became apparent that I was by far the smallest child in the class. At twelve I was no taller nor weighed more than the average nine-year-old. In my early years of schooling I was called "Cockeye" because of my crossed eyes, but in the eighth grade "Shorty" came to be my nickname.

AT FOURTEEN

## *Gambling and Stealing*

The delicatessen store was a tough grind. From early morning, when Mother cooked and served breakfasts, to midnight, when the theater crowd came in for sandwiches, it meant seventeen hours on her feet. Therefore, when she heard that my brother Abe had left Galesburg to return to St. Louis, she yielded to Sophie's appeal that I be sent back to Galesburg, and Freda remain with Tillie in Des Moines. Mother set up housekeeping for Abe, who got a good job as a bread-wagon driver, earning over twenty dollars a week. Mother, of course, hoped to have Freda and me join her in the near future in St. Louis, but it wasn't to be for quite a few years. In the first place, we children preferred the life which the smaller midwestern city affords. Selfishly we were adamant in staying away from St. Louis. Then my sister Sophie, who had no children of her own found in me a wonderful substitute. She adored me and catered to me as a mother with an only child.

So back to Galesburg I went and entered high school. Sam Sherman's business had prospered, and they had moved into a more modern flat. Now that Eli's mother went to live in Aurora with her son Dave, it left only Eli and me to share the beautiful five-room flat with the Shermans. Eli and I had a choice bedroom all to ourselves.

I enjoyed life at high school. Often when entering the candy store near the school I would be hailed as "Sheeny" or "Kike," but instead of attacking me as did the Catholic kids in St. Louis, these who called me names would in the end walk off to school with me arm in arm.

There was a great small town school spirit at Galesburg. The high schools in small towns model their activities and spirit after their neighboring colleges. This is augmented by the fact that whether it be athletics or debating, the rival teams are called upon to meet in their respective communities at alternating intervals. Before any of the big events it was customary for the entire school population to have pep rallies at the school assemblies.

Before the major contests, the assembly meeting was extended to half an hour and in the case of a "super" event, to a full hour. One such event was the football game with Rock Island High. While the boys on our team, consisting mostly of Norwegians and Swedes, were far from being lightweights, it seems, nevertheless, that they were underweight as compared to the giants on the Rock Island team. Their linemen averaged five pounds more per man.

The spirit of our school was undaunted. Never did we accept defeat until the final score. It was the day before the biggest, most contested game of the entire season with Rock Island High. A gala "pep" meeting was scheduled in the morning assembly. To depict graphically the difference in the physical proportions of both teams a boxing match was arranged on the stage of the huge auditorium. As the smallest of the 1400 students I was to represent Galesburg. Naturally they chose Dell Faulkner, the giant of our school to represent Mr. Rock Island. You guessed the outcome. Dell was knocked out by me and lay flat on the floor when I put my tiny right foot over his huge chest as victor and champion. So, were we trying to assure our audience, would be the outcome in the next day's game. Frankly, I don't remember what happened in that game with Rock Island High, but I know that if school spirit determined the outcome, we should have won.

Unfortunately, my life outside school was not to be as wholesome as in school. While I had advanced to two dollars a week for my work at the store, my bosom pal Eli was paid four dollars because he had quit school and was working full time. I resented his larger pay because even in the shorter hours I worked, my sales always ran way ahead of his. Eli was a good kid but wasn't cut out to be a salesman, while I was gifted with a powerful "line of gab." Often my sales on Saturday alone exceeded his sales for the entire week, since Saturday accounted for half the week's business. My glib sales manner made a big hit with the customers, particularly the farmers. Many would come in with their entire families, sometimes numbering half a dozen children, and insist on having nobody but the "kid" wait on them. There were two reasons for this. One, the fact that we did not conduct a one-price store, made them figure they could arrive at a fair price with an enthusiastic but naive school boy. Secondly, they wanted to "show me off" to their children pretty much in the manner of exhibiting to them a magician or a traveling medicine man who fascinated by a smooth flowing line of talk. My brother-in-law would refer glowingly to my sales exploits when recounting the day's events to my sister; but I knew it would be futile to ask him for a raise. Too often I had asked and always I had been turned down. Though I realized I had as good a home as if I had had comfortably well-off parents, the twin monsters, ambition and envy, had the best of me.

To make matters worse, several new factors of life came into my being. First I was initiated into playing pocket pool and billiards. One of my classmates at school, Howard Custer, had the privilege of playing at the exclusive Galesburg Club, where his father was a member. Soon we played hooky at least once a week to shoot pool during the afternoon. We started out playing for the fun of the game but wound up betting quarters.

About the same time I discovered that on Sundays the Seldes boys, ranging from Harry the youngest, 17, to Morris the oldest, about 30, were playing stud poker in back of their store. It was limited to eight or ten of the closest of friends and played at a nickel limit with a dime for the last card. They tried hard to keep me out, but I kept playing on the sympathy of good-natured Harry, a senior at high school, and lied about my wages being eight dollars a week. Though they were aware of my brother-in-law's frugality, they also knew that I was a slick salesman despite my "peewee" size. So in reality it was as a competing sales person rather than as a mere child that I got them to look upon me, with the result that I was admitted to the regular Sunday game.

Eli kept lending me money to take care of my losses at

pool and poker. These became quite heavy when my pool-playing friend was finally found out by his father and our pleasant excursions to the exclusive club were ended. I then turned to the regular pool halls. They wouldn't admit minors without a certificate from parents or guardian. I forged Sam Sherman's signature to a certificate and became a steady patron of the busiest pool hall in town. Now I played hooky as often as I could and spent every spare hour at the pool hall weekdays and at the poker game Sundays.

Driven to desperation by my mounting losses, which had consumed every dollar Eli had saved, it became a matter of giving up the excitement and compensation which gambling, especially with elders, afforded me, or finding a way of getting more money.

So from gambling I turned to stealing. It came about quite by accident, but I wonder if subconsciously I did not precipitate that accident. Each noon and night my brother-in-law left the store to go home for his lunch and dinner. This particular night when he was home I made a sale amounting to $5.98. By mistake I rang $3.98 on the cash register. I was prepared to ring up the additional two dollars, when in a flash it occurred to me that here was the opportunity I was looking for to get money with which to pay off Eli and continue my gambling. I took Eli into my confidence and it was agreed between us we would under-ring the cash register to the tune of ten dollars a week so we could split it between us. Working together we could stand watch for each other at the front of the store to signal the arrival of Sam.

Unfortunately it worked too well. Now I could satisfy my exhibitionist complex (which so often goes hand in hand with an inferiority complex occasioned because of physical underdevelopment) to my heart's content. I was now playing pool with the best of the shots and the biggest of the shots. I was playing fifty point straight pool or three-cushioned billiards at five dollars a game.

They showed me no quarter nor gave me any edge except that they (even the owner of the establishment) permitted me to climb the table for shots which required reach, instead of using the bridge. I had developed into a better-than-average player. In pool I could run the rack of balls quite often and it was not uncommon for me to have a high run of four or five in three cushion billiards. When I played, the game was a drawing card at the pool hall. Soon a good-sized audience would be standing around the table. Often it interfered with easy movement of the players at adjoining tables so that they hung up their cues and joined the spectators at my game. I was like the seasoned star of the stage who craves the footlights and the audience out in front, and most of all the applause.

It was thrilling to be in a darkened part of the room with only the bright lights over the green felt of the table. When my opponent was shooting, I'd be chalking up my cue in a nonchalant manner to convey the impression of being a tournament player. Looking about, I could hardly see the attire of the spectators, but only a collection of faces, intent on following with their eyes, every movement of the balls in play. My ego would reach heavenly heights when, after the completion of a spectacular shot or high run, I heard the applause of the onloookers.

Willie Hoppe, world champion billiard player and Ralph Greenleaf, champion fancy shot expert, were my idols. Nobel prize winners were nothing compared to them. Lying in my bed I would think of my high runs at the pool hall and anticipate reaching new highs in my skill the next time I played.

How news of my billiard activities reached the ears of Sophie, I never knew, but I was to taste bitter humiliation and embarrassment when one afternoon she entered the pool hall, as an uninvited guest. Apparently she made her entrance while I was enjoying the streak of a good run. In any case I was caught completely off guard. In fact, she chose the moment to make her presence known to me in a most dramatic and spirit-crushing manner. For while I was lying on the table flat on my stomach trying to execute a shot, I felt my backside being whacked by what I considered to be a cue stick. It turned out to be Sophie's umbrella. For the moment, I thought I was being attacked by some of the bad characters in the store. I was bewildered and hurt. In a moment, I recognized Sophie's voice as she poured out words of denunciation and belittlement, "You little snot-nose, you dirty little bum, you filthy little loafer, I'll teach you not to grow up into a good-for-nothing little tramp!"

Far worse than the physical hurt was the degradation and shame I felt at being exposed to my erstwhile fans as the delinquent kid I actually was, instead of the tournament player I hoped I was impressing them as being.

When I lifted myself from the table Sophie held on to her umbrella with one hand and let her other hand blindly inflict itself upon my startled face as fast and as furiously as she could maneuver it. Blood was running from my nose and onto my blouse, as, pulling me by the ear, she marched me out of the pool room.

While I was sobbing hysterically all the way home, Sophie kept preaching to me about where I would wind up doing such things and why I would always be grateful to her for saving me from a ruinous career. Through my mind kept running the question—had her informant also made known to her my Sunday poker playing activities? Too, I wondered what form the punishment would take if she learned that Eli and I were stealing from the cash register.

It was my good fortune that neither Sophie nor her

husband ever learned the worst about me until, under very happy circumstances, many years later I told them. Expressing her thanks to me for presenting her with a fur coat a few years ago, I told her it was paid for by money I "stole" from the cash register in Galesburg and told her the whole sordid business. She insisted that she didn't believe a word of it. The passing years so exalted my position with her that quite likely she always felt I had been spoofing.

For the year that I was to remain in Galesburg, I never entered a pool room again. I did, however, remain a regular Sunday poker player for a few months, until Eli and I bought our first bicycles. Neither of us had ever owned one. I had never even been on one, so I had to start learning to ride it.

I don't suppose I shall ever again experience the thrill that possession of something material can bring one, as I did when I walked out of the bicycle shop, the proud owner of a brand new, sparkling, shiny red Ranger.

The bicycles opened up a wider world for us to roam and gave us no end of thrilling experiences. First it was exciting to ride well enough to try Simmons or Prairie streets. Next we graduated to boldly challenging the heavy traffic, even on Saturdays, and proudly pedalling down Main Street. It was much fun, and healthy for my ego, to be hailed by some classmate and to lift my right hand high into the air, smile broadly and return his greeting.

Learning to ride without holding the handle bars took me weeks longer than Eli. My nervous temperament wasn't conducive to learning the art of maintaining balance on a moving vehicle. When, however, on Sundays I could follow Eli down the steep grades near the Sante Fe railroad, it was clear-cut evidence that I was a full-fledged cyclist.

During the week we planned the trips we would take on Sundays. Each week we rode to a nearby town, starting with one nearest home and finally making our longest excursion to Monmouth, Illinois. I don't believe there were any hard roads. If by chance we encountered a stretch of gravel it was even more difficult to ride on than the ordinary hardened rut in the mud roads.

Once I became a bicycle enthusiast I dropped the poker games on Sunday. Instead of sitting uncomfortably in a smoke-filled room reeking with tobacco smell, I was capitalizing on the sunshine and air of the out-of-doors. I was no longer burdened by the intensity of emotion common to those who sit around the gaming table or engage in any gambling pursuits, whether it be at the race track or stock brokerage office. Best of all, Eli and I could fall asleep no longer conscience stricken because of our stealing from the cash register. The wholesome manner to which we put out time on Sundays now reflected itself in an altogether better spirit in our work at the store. Undoubtedly it was so apparent that it resulted in my brother-in-law giving Eli a one dollar raise, and fifty cents more each week to me. Then we appeased our consciences and quit the practice of withholding any part of the cash sales.

INDIANOLA

## *An Iowa Gold Rush*

At about the time the United States entered World War I, in 1917, my wandering family was relocating.

Brother Morris failed in the grocery business in St. Louis. Brother-in-law Frank Hoffman and Sam Lundmeyer were not earning a decent living working at sewing machines. All three decided to open up shoe repair shops because some distant relative was rumored to have made good money at it.

Brother opened his shop in Des Moines, Iowa. My two brothers-in-law pooled their meager savings to buy a shop in Indianola, Iowa.

To me this wholesale moving on the part of my family was in the nature of a gold rush and I didn't want to be left out. I visited Mother in St. Louis and received her permission to move to Indianola. I had painted a rosy picture of the future this revolutionary new business had in store for me, as contrasted to my being a clerk. Of course, I was to continue school, but I could learn the business by working after school hours.

Indianola was a small town. Its population in 1918 was about three thousand people. To it, one could rightfully apply the term "typical" followed by midwestern agricultural. The business of the town was centered around the square. A solid square block in the center was neatly landscaped and had a platform in the very middle for bands, Fourth of July speakers and community get-togethers.

Surrounding the park were the four blocks containing the major share of the town's business and professional life. Here were grocers, butchers, bakers, men's haberdashers, dry goods and ladies' millinery shops. One store referred to itself as a department store. There was a fair-sized furniture store on the square, several drug and confectionery stores (with the latter the chief center of attraction for the youth of the community) and two barber shops. Lawyers and other professional men had their offices in suites on the second floor of some of the store buildings.

In addition, there were the professors and instructors from Simpson College, and retired farmers who had either prospered or grown too old. I don't believe there was a motion picture theater or any place of amusement in the town. On week days there were few Fords or teams of horses to be seen. It was desolate and one might find fewer than a dozen people walking on all four blocks of the square. Saturday afternoons were different. Then it was difficult to find a place to park one's car or to hitch one's horse and buggy. Saturday nights found most places of business packed with customers laying in their supplies for the week.

Saturday shopping in town and meeting friends and neighbors was a source of much of the farmers' families' social life and entertainment. This was supplemented by Sunday's meeting in church and at socials Sunday night. Occasionally one would go to Des Moines to shop at the big stores and see a movie.

I became acquainted with this simple, wholesome life in the summer of 1918. I never went to school in Indianola because at the end of the summer I was certain my restless nature could not endure the small-town life. In the sixty days I was there I did nothing but work at the shoe repair shop. The routine was the same every day. After an early breakfast my brothers-in-law and I would walk to the shoe repair shop off the square on a side street. We opened a few minutes before eight o'clock to be able to do a few "while-you-wait" jobs before schools and stores opened for business. In a matter of minutes I was taught how to take a freshly-soled or heeled shoe and do the finishing job. That simply meant the holding of the shoe sidewise up against the speedy revolving emery wheel which shaved it down to a fairly smooth surface. The sandpaper wheel would then finish the job of taking off the slightest trace of any rough edges. The next operation was the application of liquid polish, and finally the polished surfaces were applied to the revolving brush.

I had to be very careful not to let the shoe slip when doing the emery wheel or sandpaper operation. In case of a slip, my hand or fingers could be badly hurt. With the revolving brush, it was different. I could push the shoe into it with abandon and if it made contact with my hand I would only feel as if my hand were tickled.

It gave me a feeling of manliness to be doing such work and I nagged my brother-in-law until he permitted me to do every job except hand-work or machine-stitching. Putting on rubber heels was a cinch. I liked that job best of all. The thrill, however, was in stitching a new sole on a pair of shoes. I trained on some discarded shoes until I became good enough to take a chance on customers' shoes. Sole-stitching, however, was my nemesis, because it required more height to hold the shoe properly and far more strength than my ninety pounds could muster, to do the job right. That is why they forbade me to do any shoe stitching. Sam handled all the hat cleaning and blocking alone. His experience in a cap factory qualified him for that department.

During the week I did all the shoe shining. On Saturdays the barber's son from next door worked for us as a shoeshine boy. On Saturday afternoons when the town was full the six chairs of the shoeshine stand were put to good use. From four to ten at night we went at a steady pace. Sam and Frank did little repair work because they too would have to shine shoes. That business was extra profitable because polish cost so little. The dime we got was nine cents gross profit. If we did one hundred and twenty pairs, it meant twelve dollars less two dollars paid to the barber boy. In addition, half of the shines might produce nickel tips, so that roughly thirteen dollars clear profit was realized on Saturday's shoeshining business.

The Victrola would be going all the while we were shining. Most customers knew the collection of records as well as we did and requested those they liked. We never bought any new records but used only those that came with the purchase of the shop. "K-K-K-Katy, Beautiful Katy, You're the Only Girl for Me" was the favorite. "Alexander's Ragtime Band" was pretty high on the hit parade of our customers.

At ten we drew down the green window shades. We finished the few shines on the stand, and the customers left. At about ten-fifteen we took a few cold bottles of soda pop from the ice box in the rear and refreshed ourselves before counting the day's receipts and figuring the earnings for the week. They weren't much. Every day wasn't Saturday. Shines during the week were almost nil. Two, three dollars at the most. From hat cleaning and blocking we might realize about thirty dollars to thirty-five dollars a week. Shoeshines about twenty dollars and shoe repairing ninety dollars. Out of the gross income there were royalties to be paid for the use of the machinery. There were machinery parts and needles to pay for. Needles were quite an item because so often they would break while stitching. There was rent and a whopping electric bill for the power used by the machinery. Chiefly, of course, there was the cost of the leather and incidental materials used for shoe repairing and hat blocking, so that a gross intake of one hundred and forty dollars a week left little over sixty-five dollars a week on which both families could live.

The rising cost of living brought about by the war made it very tough going. I remember the ingenuity exercised by my sisters in stretching those food dollars to the limit. Their object was to prepare meals of foodstuffs that cost the least and filled the stomach the most. The prize dish concocted to achieve that purpose was a bread-and-potato pudding. They would buy stale white bread at the bakery shop, soak the bread in water, combine it with grated potatoes and some flour, and then they baked a large pudding about fifteen inches in diameter. Hardly a day passed that we didn't have this pudding as a "filler" at the evening meal. Life in Indianola was far from a gold rush.

HIGH SCHOOL SENIOR

## *A Year of Great Happiness*

Morris was doing much better in the shoe repair shop in Des Moines. Instead of waiting to do "while-you-wait" jobs when the soldiers from nearby Camp Dodge came to town, he went to their barracks and lugged back sacks full of shoes for repair. Morris was doing well and wanted me to come to live and work with him. I was delighted to make the change because Indianola was too dull to suit me.

In September 1918, I enrolled as a senior in North Des Moines High School. When Tillie moved to Indianola, Freda moved in to live with my sister-in-law Lena on Bluff Street. It was a lovely six-room bungalow and not too crowded for Morris, Lena, their two baby boys, Freda and myself. Lena treated us as if we were her own children. Anything she did for her boys she would do for us.

The deal with Morris was that he was to pay me five dollars a week after school and I was to retain all tips received from shoeshining.

I was never happier in my life. That year before I was graduated from North High was in many respects the best of my childhood. I cannot recall a negative note in the course of living that year. My eyes had finally straightened after years of religiously wearing eyeglasses. My acne, however, still persisted even beyond my teens. I was still a midget, weighing under one hundred pounds, and under five feet tall at sixteen years of age. Instead of being a handicap, my size served to provide me with extra opportunities for fun. Not the least of these was the fact that beautiful girls knowing me to be sexually harmless took liberties in kidding which they would never do with a potential "he-man." In exchange for help I might give them in their history or English, they might playfully and innocently kiss me on the cheek and say, "What a darling you are." Of course they would not be so bold with a fellow whom they might want as a date. I was sexually immature, but appreciated being kissed by a pretty girl just the same.

Everyone was nice to me because I struck them as a cute, grammar-school kid who for some freak reason was included in their group. They were particularly intrigued by the fact that an endless volume of glib talk would emanate from my vocal cords. Under my picture in the 1919 *Oracle*, official yearbook of the school, was written: "The one and only trial of Sam's senior year was being shoved out of freshman classrooms and told to go to grammar school where he belonged. Sam has much to say but it is worthwhile listening to him."

It pleased me to walk along the corridors between classes and be greeted by virtually everyone that passed. "How ya, Sammy!" and "Hello, Sammy!" were always accompanied by wide smiles and glances that assured me I was well-liked. Though I worked after school hours and Saturdays, my brother permitted me to be absent the half dozen Saturdays during the football season. I was a combination cheerleader and water boy.

I was on most intimate terms with all the football players. Big, burly Curtis Morton, a Negro fullback of our team, could win a prize in a "most beautiful teeth" contest. When he smiled at you with his big dimples, flashing eyes and pearly white teeth, in contrast to his black skin, you knew you were being smiled at. Glen Lowe, our quarterback, was agile and swift on the football field and also with the girls of the school. I suppose he could have had his pick of any girl in the school except Cloris Wallace. She was smart, beautiful and had Joyce Allen as her beau. He was the captain of the football team, the most popular man in school and my idol.

The two girls I selected as the most beautiful, whom I secretly made love to, whose every step I literally followed every chance I had, were Cloris Wallace and Ione Hanks. If they read this it will come as a complete surprise to them. Cloris was my number one "pin-up" girl and Ione a close second. For many months I doubt if ever I went to bed at night without spending endless moments imagining one or the other as my sweetheart.

Even as a dream it took colossal nerve to conjure such thoughts in my mind when they were out-of-this-world beauties and sought after by the most eligible, while I was, in the vernacular, a "sawed-off, pint-sized runt." But as the words of that song so aptly put it, "You couldn't stop me from dreaming."

Cloris was about five feet tall. She wore her blond hair parted in the center and had the bluest of blue eyes. Dark eyelashes were in sharp contrast to her fair peach-like complexion. The natural tint of a pinkishness in her cheeks, together with the lusciousness of her kiss-inviting lips completed the picture of extravagant yet wholesome beauty, the like of which I have seldom seen.

Ione was several inches taller than Cloris. She had jet black hair and dark brown eyes. She had a slight dimple in her chin. Her skin was almost milkwhite, which in contrast to her dark hair and eyes, was sufficient to make her breathtaking to look at. Frankly, I can't remember so clearly in her case, as I had far less contact with her, whether it was make-up or nature-endowed color in her cheeks and lips. In any case, to me she appeared too beautiful to be real. If I preferred Cloris it was because she was more my height and I knew her to speak to; while the most I ever received from Ione was a broad smile.

That year was an extraordinary one for our school. Our football team not only won the championship of the city's three high schools, but also won the State championship. The statistics in the 1919 *Oracle* show something of an all-time record to that date in that no team ever scored against us.

The year was also an extraordinary one for me. It was the one and only year during my childhood and youth that was spent in wholesome and something approaching normal living.

HIGH SCHOOL GRADUATION

## *Climbing the Ladder of Success*

In June 1919 Freda and I were graduated from high school. Mother came from St. Louis and Sophie from Galesburg. It was an extraordinary event because no other members of our family had even completed grammar school. I went to Frankel Clothing store on Walnut Street and bought a fine serge suit with short knickerbocker trousers. The three high schools then in Des Moines combined graduation exercises, which were held at the Coliseum. Of the hundreds who received their diplomas, I was the only one among the boys who wasn't wearing long pants.

On the platform, while waiting my turn to be called to receive my diploma, I could see my entire family seated among the huge audience, but they couldn't see me until I stepped down in front when my name was called. I then saw the female members of my family burst into tears. After the exercises I asked Mother and my sisters what made them cry. They replied that it would be difficult for a youngster like myself, reared in America, to understand and appreciate the great value they placed on our acquiring high school diplomas. To them it signified that the hopes and dreams they brought with them from Russia had come to full fruition. Indeed they were tears of joy, tears of promise, tears of gratitude to the land that made it possible.

My senior year at "high" was a momentous one. It was the year in which I made rapid strides in developing into a salesman, and which culminated in opening a business of my own.

My work began after I left school about three-thirty. At six I went home with my brother to have dinner and return about six forty-five to work until nine. I gave scant attention to home work and miraculously got by with better than passing grades in dull subjects and very high grades in those I enjoyed. Before important exams I would not return to the store but remained home to do last minute cramming.

Our store was called the Modern Shoe Repair Shop. Directly opposite was the City Market. There could be found the choicest fruits. I stuffed myself with whatever fruit was in season. The black cherry and seedless grape seasons found me a glutton. It was nothing for me to eat a pound of each in an afternoon. I wonder whether my stomach ulcers can be traced to the large doses of acid in fruits to which I exposed myself at that time!

Our patrons were exclusively the officers and soldiers who came to town from Camp Dodge to have a good time. Rarely did they fail to tip. Many tipped a dime, and a

The smiling Goldfarbs—Gene, Sam, Alan and Murray.

Tried long pants in 1919. Upper classmen at Washington University forced him to wear knee pants until 1921.

The author (left), with his pal Lou Gruber, at the University of Chicago Law School, year 1924.

A portion of graduation class was combined with East and West High. Sammy Goldfarb, Age 16½, only boy in knee pants.

quarter was not uncommon when it was a combination job of shoes and officer's leather puttees. At the end of the day I would find my tips around three dollars, so that with a big Saturday and five dollar base wage I would have over twenty-five dollars a week.

A few months after I came to work for Morris he decided to put in a line of soldiers' dress shoes and leggings. The latter were either canvas which were put together by drawing a cord through hooks, or the woolen ones that wrapped around the legs. Enlisted men were issued only the extra heavy, crude hobnail shoes, so that they were eager for the visits to town to wear dress shoes. It was a success from the start; we received sixty pairs as an opening shipment one Thursday afternoon and by Saturday evening they were all sold out at about twelve dollars a pair. This made shoeshining and repairing a shabby business by comparison.

My experience in Galesburg soon made itself evident to my brother, who hired a colored boy to take care of the shine stand and put me to clerking on a straight twenty-five dollar a week salary. This was good pay for a boy. Outside of a few dollars I spent during the week for fruit and candy, haircuts and clothes on rare occasions, I was able to save most of my earnings as I had no board to pay. By Christmas of 1918 I had saved over three hundred dollars.

Fortunately I was not exposed to the temptation of losing any money playing pool or poker. I had completely forgotten about this sordid aspect of my life. In Des Moines I had wholesome substitutes for the vices which I indulged in while living in Galesburg. In the first place I was earning good pay. I had my Saturday liberties for football games, which I never had had previously. Finally, and most significant, was the fact that I had a group of nice fellows to associate with Sundays and holidays. Add up the circumstances and it makes it easy to understand why I was a bad boy in Galesburg and a wholesome lad in Des Moines.

Business boomed after the Armistice on November 11, 1918. Instead of the soldiers discarding their army attire and changing to civilian clothes, they bought the best military clothes they could obtain. They wanted to return to their home towns looking like officers.

This was especially true when the boys from overseas were discharged. They wanted to get out of their ill-fitting uniforms, hobnailed shoes, dirty hats and worn leggings. They wanted everything new and better fitting.

Then I had an idea. Instead of clerking for my brother I wanted to install a concession of other type merchandise in his store. Morris said it would be O.K. He permitted me to install a small showcase where I carried a line of soldiers' insignia and silk hat-cords. I was to continue to sell shoes and leggings as I had been doing, but instead of drawing twenty-five dollars a week I would draw no salary at all. The profit on the showcase merchandise was to be my sole compensation. Early in January I received my initial stock of insignia and cords. They sold as fast as lightning. It was only a question of getting them fast enough. On December 18, 1918 I was sixteen. A month later I cleared as much as eighty dollars profit in a single week. My average profit was about sixty-five dollars each week. A terrible conflict raged in my heart and mind for many days. On the one hand I wanted my brother with a family to procure the profit now accruing to me, and on the other hand I was reluctant to go back to the nominal weekly wage. Happily, I resolved this problem. I sublet a part of a candy store in another location and sold similar merchandise to that of my brother's. During the year I made over three thousand dollars.

ALTOONA, IOWA

## *Life in An Agricultural Village*

Life in 1919 in Des Moines was a time of awakening for me. I was a high school graduate, and a successful merchant. And yet physically and spiritually I was a boy of thirteen rather than the youth of seventeen. Toward September, business showed signs of dying, so turning my thoughts to the future I decided to stay in business only long enough to liquidate my stock and work toward going to college. This presented no problem for now it was certain I would fulfill the dream of my childhood and go to Washington University in St. Louis. However, I missed the opportunity to enroll that fall, so I decided to postpone my college career for a year.

In late November when I closed my store, my brother Morris became a bosom friend of his erstwhile competitor, Jacob Shames. The two of them became partners and purchased a general store in Altoona, Iowa, about twenty-five miles from Des Moines. They prevailed upon me to work for them at the lucrative wage of thirty dollars a week. While I had been earning far more in my business, I had the good sense to realize that a boy in knee pants was unlikely to earn nearly as much elsewhere.

It was a long, tough grind each day, working in the general store in Altoona. Morris and his partner alternated each week opening the store. The store was opened at eight o'clock, which meant getting up at six to allow for dressing, breakfast, the walk to the interurban station and an hour's ride to Altoona. The biting cold often registered below zero and froze the potatoes and bananas in the store. Then we would get up at three to make the four forty-five a.m. train. In that way we could still keep the fire alive in the furnace and the store warm enough to protect perishable produce. Since they were heads of families, while I was a carefree youth, I insisted and got consent to relieve them of the five o'clock openings during the cold spells.

It gave me a feeling of adequacy, of being an adult, to arise a little after three in the morning, clean up and prepare a simple breakfast of fruit juice, cold cereal and a glass of milk. I was well prepared to challenge the howling winds and deep snowdrifts outdoors. I wore long-sleeve, ankle-length woolen underwear. This I covered with a sleeveless woolen sweater and heavy flannel wool shirt. The socks were woolen. Thick leather, army-style shoes were covered by high felt-lined galoshes. Finally I put on my heavy, plaid, belted mackinaw coat and cap to match. Pulling down the ear-muffs, and tying them with string under my chin, I would bravely venture forth into the dark streets that were heavily snow laden and serenely quiet, ready to pit myself against the vicissitudes of nature's elements.

Trudging through the snow long before dawn, creating the first footprints perhaps a foot or more deep with every step I took, made me feel like an arctic explorer. I often thought of my friends sound asleep, living quiet normal lives. Tracing my life since Father's death, revealed to me how unsettled and abnormal it was compared to the lives of my friends. Moments of self-pity were mingled with moments of pride of achievement. I envied them their sheltered existence, free of worry and care and assured of a successful future. Above all, I envied them for the clean, wholesome lives they had led as contrasted to my sinful days of stealing and pool-playing. It never occurred to me that they were anything less than angelic while I was burdened by an unbearable weight of a guilt complex added to the inferiority of my retarded physical development. Thank God I was no longer cross-eyed!

When I reached the store I would lose no time in firing the basement furnace. When I had the fire going I would make a bed of burlap sacks and sleep on the floor until it was time to open the store at eight. By then Mr. Shames and my brother would arrive and I had a sense of satisfaction that I was making it possible for them to get their normal rest.

Farmers would come in to shop as soon as the store opened. Many came into the store with no thought of buying anything but to spend an hour or two sitting around the grate where the hot air from the furnace rose. We supplied them with chairs and they made themselves comfortable in a conversational grouping. Some chewed tobacco. But whether they were gum or tobacco chewers they were all spitters. Soon Mr. Shames cut down considerably the amount of spitting into the furnace grate by placing a couple of extra large spittoons around the grate and posting a sign urging that for sanitary reasons they please expectorate in the spittoons. They all meant to abide by the request but every now and then one would revert to habit and spit down the furnace.

One side of the store was given to groceries, meats and produce. The other side carried the stock of shoes, dry goods and clothing for men, women and children. My brother managed the food department and Mr. Shames took charge of the other departments. They had a clerk in the food department, and I assisted Mr. Shames. On the whole, it was a dull, unprofitable business in contrast to the booming business we had experienced in catering to the soldiers in Des Moines.

DOLORES AND DIANA

## *My Introduction to Fornication*

In April I yielded to my mother's plea and with my sister Freda left for St. Louis to make a home with Mother and to enter into a new phase of living.

For Freda it was to mean no further schooling but embarkation on a secretarial career. For me, it meant fulfillment of a childhood dream—admittance to Washington University. I had to wait until September 1920 to enroll, so in the meantime I joined Freda in a job hunt. She was hired as a stenographer at the office of the Bierman Company, junk dealers on North Twelfth Street. They also had another business, the sale of tires and tubes on Thirty-third and Locust streets, and I was hired as the sole person in charge. The reason for my unique job was the fact that what was normally a heavy automobile traffic street was now completely without traffic. Due to some political scandal the streets were torn up. They were stacked for miles with wooden paving blocks, but no work was being done. This situation lasted for many months, from mid-April past September when I quit the job to enroll in college. Days passed without a single customer to disturb my newly developed reading habit.

My sister collected many old back issues of magazines at the junk yard where she was employed. Old copies of the Literary Digest, Saturday Evening Post and countless detective story magazines comprised my range of reading. I liked best of all the Octavius Roy Cohen series depicting life of the colored people in the larger cities of the South.

On the whole it was a dull, uninteresting job that

afforded me no opportunity to learn the tire business. Contact with Ike Bierman, my employer, was irregular and rare. Two or three times a week he would drop in to see if I was asleep. The twenty dollars weekly wage was in effect payment for being a watchman rather than a salesman. For a change, climaxed by the tough winter in Altoona, the spring and summer loafing job with the Royal Tire Company was not altogether unwelcome.

When summer rolled around I would lower the awning on the Locust Street side and park myself in a chair in front of the store to do my reading. That's how I came to know my neighbors, Dolores and Diana, who lived in the duplex flat adjoining our store. Around noon one or the other would come out of the flat with an undersized bull dog. Both Dolores and Diana were cordial in their daily greeting. Dolores, about forty-five, had a face very much like the dog she took out for its airing. I don't mean to be facetious or unkind in making that comparison, for subsequently other fellows, without any encouragement from me, referred to her as "dog face." Always in colorful negligees, high-heeled satin bedslippers and faces made up, the ladies alternated in their caring for the dog's need for the outdoors. They would not have been so decollete, I'm sure, if it were not for their knowledge that there was no traffic and rarely any person passing on the sidewalk.

Diana was young and beautiful. Her fiery red hair, milk white skin and greenish-blue eyes tantalized me from the first time I saw her. After several greetings from Diana I picked up enough courage to walk over to her under the pretense of currying favor with the dog.

Then I inhaled the aroma of her perfume and since I had never known of its existence I assumed it was the natural smell of her body. I was driven to new heights of ecstasy and wonderment. She was the most alluring creature on earth to my naive and boyish understanding.

Truly she didn't strike me as being of this world. She didn't seem real but rather like some mystic, Grecian goddess of old. I counted it a most thrilling experience and treat to be permitted to stand near her as she paused to let the dog raise one of its hind legs to a tree. We hardly spoke. For me it was sufficient to feast my eyes on this red-headed charmer. "Out of this world" Diana was arousing every current of red, surging blood that was coarsing through the boy then turning to a young man—me, at eighteen.

The passing days found me incapable of eating, sleeping or reading without her on my mind. I spent hours in anticipation of what it would feel like to hold her in my arms and kiss her. I took her to be about my age, but subsequently learned she was twenty. I felt certain she would reject any suggestion of going to the soda parlor, movies or spending Sunday in the park. I was about to give it up as a lost cause, when I became aroused one day as she simply asked, "What's your name?" My heart was gladdened and hysterical. I was inspired sufficiently not only to ask her name but bold enough to ask whether she would mind if I went indoors to talk to her. My dreams of the past days reached fulfillment when she gleefully replied, "Sure, why not?" My excitement was so great I left the store doors wide open, completely forgetting my responsibility to my job. Such was the way of a sensuous youth, far more naive and retarded than most other boys, and a maid, exotic and wise in the ways of the world.

Entrance to the abode of Dolores and Diana was a heartpounding experience. No bridegroom has ever felt greater emotional ecstasy and mystery in carrying his bride over the threshold of the honeymoon cottage than I did when the door behind Diana, the dog and me was shut. Always finding it difficult to breathe easily, I could nevertheless smell the sweetest smells and see the most beautiful coloring I had ever seen as I was ushered into the living room. I was dazzled by the interior of Diana's home. Mirrors everywhere on the walls, made the ordinary sized rooms look tremendous. It was a delight to the eyes to take in at one sweep the various pastel colors of the furniture and drapes. A profuse use of lace on the backs and sides of the upholstered pieces and on top of commodes all combined to give the effect of splendor and was in keeping with the impression Diana made on me. It was fitting that this goddess should live in such heavenly quarters or so at least did it appear to me at the time.

Sheepishly and yokel-like I veered myself to one of the heavily cushioned chairs and without invitation plumped myself down in it. Diana, however, asked me to come to her bedroom.

I leaped from my chair with joy, for it was dawning on me that my yearning to kiss Diana was nearing the realm of probability. Surely, I reasoned, she couldn't be too offended if I attempted only the mildest of pecks—just a kiss on the cheek perhaps—if she is so friendly as to invite me to her room.

No sooner did we get to her room, when Diana kicked off her pumps, removed her beautiful negligee, and seated on her bed before me was the fairy princess of my dreams covered only in an eye captivating, pink chemise. Before I could grasp the significance of this extraordinary familiarity Diana asked, "What do you say, Kid, what do you want to do?"

I was stunned. I didn't know what to say. Here I had dreamed and planned for the moment when I could steal a kiss from this elegant creature and now when so simply she asked me what I wanted, I found myself gripped with fear and uncertainty. I no longer felt the urge to kiss or embrace Diana as I had wanted so passionately to do for many days. I was bewildered. I felt the urge to run away.

Diana must have understood. "Honey, ain't you ever made love to a woman?" she asked. Then in a flash it came to me—the competitors in Des Moines who brought women to my store; the words "whore" and "prostitute" I had heard boys use contemptuously. So this was what a whore was—a female who lacked a sense of shame and required no coaxing or overtures to be kissed and embraced.

I don't recall what, if any, words were exchanged. The next thing I remember was Diana unbuttoning the fly of my pants, urging me and helping me to undress. She was the master of the situation. Then, while I was still in a semi-hypnotic state, she initiated me into my first act of fornication.

I felt ashamed and wanted to run away from the scene of my degradation. When Diana spoke to me I couldn't open my mouth to reply. When she had given me a hygienic treatment I hurriedly dressed and made ready to leave, but she reached out her hand to me. I thought it was an invitation to shake hands, to appease my sulking mood, which must have been apparent to her. I offered my hand to her and she let out a loud burst of laughter, which continued off and on until she saw me to the door. She paused to tell me that while it was nice to get my "maiden head" she was not doing it for free. She went on to explain that she charged various prices for her services, but because I was a good kid and neighbor, she wanted only two dollars from me. When I paid her she escorted me downstairs. There we spotted Dolores in the living room. Dolores smiled and asked me to come back again. In the meantime, much to my embarrassment Diana laughingly told her how I expected to be given a handshake and be thanked for giving her the privilege of initiating me to sex.

It felt good to breathe the air of the outdoors. I ran to

the store next door and was grateful to find everything intact. I went to look in the mirror over the sink at the rear of the store to see if I had changed because of the experience I had just had. I felt I had done a great wrong and that I should never again be the same person.

WASHINGTON UNIVERSITY

## *A Dream Fulfilled*

At last the long wait was over and the day had come to enter college at Washington University in September 1920. I entered the School of Commerce and Finance.

Faintly I remember Professors Cullen in economics, and Edgar James Swift in psychology. Professor Krebs taught accounting and had as an assistant for the course a recent graduate, Walter Goldman. In my freshman year there was an associate professor by the name of Hollingsworth. He taught political science to a class of several hundred students. Often the class would stamp their feet on the floor to a point where Hollingsworth was unable to maintain control. He was a nice chap but for some reason the students took advantage of him.

Regrettably I cannot recall to mind the images, to say nothing of the names, of any of the others on the faculty who taught me during my three years at Washington.

College life was uneventful and drab for me. In my freshman year I was subjected to much hazing because I was the only boy on the campus in knee pants. Others might pass off as upper classmen, but if I failed to wear the traditional green cap the paddling squad would take care of me properly!

I enjoyed the time I spent at the gymnasium. There, for the first time, I was initiated into running on an indoor rubber track, also playing in the enclosed handball courts.

I was poor in all athletics. When we engaged in the compulsory mile or longer runs on the outdoor track, I was always the last to come in. At handball I was always beaten but thoroughly enjoyed playing, though I seldom found anyone willing to play with me. My accounting instructor, Walter Goldman, and his younger brother Lawrence, a pre-medical student, were among the best players and often played with me through sympathy. They sensed my predicament and exercised unusual kindness and understanding. They were extraordinary boys from an extraordinary family.

Many boys earned their room and board at the dormitories by acting as waiters in the mess hall. Several of my friends worked a full eight hours on the night shift of the Post Office. Dave Crystal and Meyer Roudman were two who pursued this rugged grind.

The latter two and I were the only three students at Washington who came from the Gamble Street ghetto. They worked at night while I worked after school hours.

My brother Morris and a Mr. Morris Broida started to manufacture ladies house dresses. I did the bookkeeping. The factory occupied the rear portion of a sixth floor loft at 905 Washington Avenue. Altogether the loft was six thousand square feet.

My firm traded as the Central Garment Manufacturing Company. The idea of starting a house dress business came to my brother and Mr. Broida while they were in Oklahoma. Mr. Broida ran a shoe store and my brother a general dry goods store. Both disliked living in small towns and decided to merge their capital in a joint venture in St. Louis. So in 1921 I was initiated into the business which I was to follow consistently thereafter until this day.

To supplement my income of twenty dollars a week as bookkeeper for Central I conceived the idea of selling clothes to students. The idea was to bring them down to the neighboring Pollock's Clothing factory and earn five dollars on every suit I sold. In that way the purchaser still saved money, because the retail profit on a suit of clothes was about twelve dollars to fifteen dollars. Through me they would buy at wholesale, plus an extra two or three dollars, which the manufacturer took for his trouble, and five dollars for my commission.

I embarked on a strong advertising campaign, using as a sole medium the bulletin board of the men's recreation room at school. "Save money on your clothes by buying direct from the factory" was my steady punch-line. I sold about two suits a week for some time.

One day when I came to the bulletin board to put up a new sign I found pasted across my old sign a Barney Google comic strip. It showed Barney Google arranging a deal with a friend in the wholesale clothing business. Barney was to get five dollars on every suit he sold. Next it showed Barney commenting on the fine fit, as one of his customers was trying on a suit. Then he ordered, "Now look here, Henry, I want this friend of mine to get this suit absolutely wholesale—understand, absolutely wholesale." Later it showed Barney returning to get his commission, which the merchant refused to give because he took Barney at his word and gave the customer the real wholesale price.

I tore down the comic strip, but every day a fresh copy of the Google strip was pinned on the bulletin board. I never did learn who did it, but it did serve to destroy my business.

At that time Washington University had two Jewish students of extraordinary ability who were destined to do great work for their professions and communities. They were Abe Sachar and Israel Treiman. Both won Rhodes scholarships to study in England. Treiman was a professor of law at Washington University. Abe Sachar is president of Brandeis University.

In my third year at Washington I flunked college algebra and decided to quit school.

## MIRACULOUS PHYSICAL DEVELOPMENT

### *First Sexual Affair*

My home life was rather unbalanced as there was no cohesion of thought or action on the part of Mother, sister Freda and myself. We went our separate ways. Mother, though poor herself, was busily engaged in countless charitable endeavors. Freda was now a grown young lady of twenty-one, working as a secretary and mixing socially with men and women of voting age. I was left pretty much on my own.

When I was in my sophomore year at college, my brother's firm merged with National Skirt and Dress Company and operated under the latter's name. Now they occupied the full six thousand feet of loft space. Mr. Broida and my brother felt they could benefit by the technical experience of I. D. Goldberg and the latter took a liking to the housedress business. Since National had a good bookkeeper, my new job was to sell after school in the city of St. Louis and vicinity.

As if by a miracle, I grew six inches in my eighteenth year, so I considered myself a man. Now for the first time I felt I was not intruding when I attended parties or went to affairs of college students at the Y.M.H.A. On rare occasions I visited a house of prostitution, but for the most part my energies were consumed by schooling, work and new-found social activities.

My first sexual "affair" was with one of the girls working as an examiner in the factory. Coming down the elevator with her one day after work I made a date to take her to the movies that night. She was a plain-looking girl but she had a show-girl figure. When I called for her that evening and saw her dressed up, I was dazzled by her stunning appearance. I took her for a soda after the movies, then suggested a spot in the park where we could "talk." It was no conquest. Like a ripe apple, about to fall from the tree, she was eager and ready to give herself to me. As sensuous and passionate as I must have been, I had the consideration and moral scruples to make certain she was no virgin by bluntly asking her. Having her assurance, I experienced for the first time the thrill of sexual relationship with one who hungered for it as I did. Thereafter for many months I saw her several times a week. In the summers it was in the park. In winter or inclement weather it was a room at a lodging house. This steady gratification gave me better balance.

TRAVELING SALESMAN

## *I Learn to Treat All Females As Ladies*

In the summer of 1922 I made the first selling trip of my life on the road. When I was nineteen years old I bought a Ford roadster on credit, and became a traveling salesman. I planned a trip southwest from St. Louis to Oklahoma where I would cover the eastern half of the state. I was anxious to visit my brother Abe and my sisters Lottie and Tillie, who had stores in Oklahoma.

I was interested, of course, in seeing how well I would do as a traveling salesman, but above all I looked forward to amorous adventure for I had heard fascinating stories about the good times salesmen had in "making women" while traveling on the road.

So with a light heart and a head full of the imaginary escapades I hoped to encounter, I started out on my first venture as a traveling salesman.

After dining in the hotel coffee shop I sat in the lobby reading the evening paper. A few chairs away I noticed a young man who looked familiar to me, and I walked over to ask whether he was from St. Louis. He was Milton Frank, selling ladies' novelty shoes for a St. Louis firm by the name of David Wohl. We exchanged a few ideas and he welcomed the thought of traveling with me as far as Tulsa, Oklahoma. He carried but one sample case containing about twenty single shoes.

I shall never forget how on the following day we entered a general store together and I stood while Milton approached the store owner. "Frank is the name," he said, "I represent the Wohl Shoe Company of St. Louis." Not what he said, but his poised and assured manner of saying it impressed me. He had an air of feeling cocksure of himself, and he was. By his introductory remarks he transmitted the feeling to the prospective buyer that he was a bearer of good things, that the buyer was privileged to meet him. The years have proven that he was right in that attitude, for his company has become one of the largest in America.

From Sedalia we worked our way to what I shall call "Paris," Kansas, where we spent the night at the leading hotel. Having Milton's companionship I found it easy to keep my mind off women, particularly since he impressed me as not being interested in them. As far as I could observe, he was all business and no "monkey" business.

The following morning in the hotel I was to experience as frightening an escapade as ever I have had in my life. After breakfast in the coffee shop I went out to call on the merchants with three or four of my best styles under my arm. The idea was to flash extra good numbers at the buyers and if they were interested, to return later with the complete line. About ten forty-five I had covered the merchants and returned to the hotel to get the remaining samples. Entering the lobby, which was desolate at that time of the day, I put my dresses down on a chair while I went to the desk to ask for my mail. A gentleman gave me a letter from my firm, which I opened and started to read nonchalantly as I walked to pick up my samples. When I came to the chair where I had left them I saw a handsome woman of about thirty-five peeking at the dresses. "They are lovely," she said. Spontaneously I answered, "Yes, they are, but if you want to see more beautiful styles, come to my room with me."

No sooner said than done! She came along with me to my room and entered before me. I left the door open. She immediately closed the door. This gave me the idea that she was interested in having a sex escapade. I proceeded to show her all my samples. She looked at them admiringly and I asked her which she liked best. She picked three or four as her choice. I said, "You can have them if you go to bed with me." By her silence I could see that she was surprised at my crude offer. "Pardon me," she said, "will you repeat what you just said?" So once again I said, "You can have these dresses if you go to bed with me." Then commanding the sweetest and coyest manner, she replied, "Maybe—but before I do I must tell you this. Remember the big strapping giant of a man who handed you the mail at the desk? That's Mr. X, my husband. I'll just telephone downstairs and find out whether it is all right with him." In a second she was at the telephone talking. Fortunately for me, Mr. X was out. This I learned when Mrs. X said, "Tell him to come to room 202 as soon as he returns from the bank."

I started pleading with the lady. I brought up the fact that I left the door open and she closed it. Her explanation was, "I don't want the chambermaids making a practice of going into salesmen's rooms to look at their samples." She then went on to paint a picture of what Mr. X would do to me for the insult to his wife. She mentioned the fact that in Oklahoma where they ran a boarding house Mr. X once shot a drunken Indian because of an insult to her. "He was drunk and an Indian, while you are sober and white," she added.

Seeing that I could not appease her I did not bother to take any of my belongings but fled from the room like a madman. I decided to leave my car in the garage for a few days while I got out of town. Fortunately, as I was headed for the interurban station to get the train for Nowata, Oklahoma, right across the border from Kansas, I ran into Milton. I told him to get the car, pick up my belongings and samples and meet me at the Campbell Hotel, Nowata. I gave him no time to ask questions.

I was agreeably surprised to find that Milton brought all of my things to Nowata later in the afternoon when he completed his business. I did not sleep too well for several nights after that because that was the period when the Ku Klux Klan was riding high and I felt they would join Mr. X in coming after me. This narrow escape from whatever Mr. X might have chosen to do with me served to impress me with the stupidity of the crude, blunt approach to a female.

BOOM-TIME, OKLAHOMA!

## *I Lose My Pants and Run into the K.K.K.*

I was dazzled by my first glimpse of the downtown business section of Tulsa. The Tulsa Hotel, then the leading in the state, was a beehive of activity. From the large number of big-brimmed cowboy Stetson hats one could ascertain the fact that oil and cattlemen made it their headquarters. All kinds of fantastic stories were told about the extraordinary spending and gambling on the part of the oil men.

It was the old story of "easy come, easy go." Many who had been poor farmers became millionaires overnight as oil was struck on their property. The atmosphere of the hotel was enough to excite any visitor. That is why I decided to make the Tulsa Hotel the base of my selling operations in the state. I worked out of Tulsa during the week but returned to it for the weekends.

My first weekend in Tulsa Hotel resulted in another embarrassing situation for me. I got into a poker game with some salesmen I met through Mr. Max Broida, a brother of one of my bosses. The game wound up in my room, where I played "freeze out" with a Mr. Drexel of Kansas City. After losing all the money I had for traveling expenses, I lost my watch to him. I took him seriously when he put up ten dollars against my pants and he won those too! I was traveling with only one suit and could not leave my room because he took my pants with him. There I was in my room with no money, no watch and no trousers. Since I couldn't leave, I kept calling the rooms of Messrs. Broida and Drexel. Finding them out, I kept paging them in the lobby. Several hours later Mr. Broida came to my room with my trousers and watch, which he returned to me with the understanding that I was to return to him the thirty-five dollars which he paid to Drexel. I called St. Louis and spoke to Mr. Goldberg, my brother's partner, because I did not dare divulge such matters to my brother. Goldberg took it good-naturedly and wired me money to clear up my debts and continue my traveling.

Leaving Tulsa, I stopped in Drumright, about fifty-five miles west, where I visited my cousins. They drove me to Shamrock, only six miles south, on a terrible dirt road. Here for the first time I saw oil derricks by the thousands. They were so close together that it looked as if one could step from one to another.

It was late in the afternoon when we reached Shamrock Mercantile Company, the dry goods and clothing store owned by my brother Abe and brother-in-law Frank Hoffman.

My folks were as thrilled to see me as I was to see them. It came as a most agreeable surprise for me to see such a heavily stocked store of good merchandise. They had taken two twenty foot stores and broken through to give them a forty foot front by about eighty in depth. They had a complete line of apparel for men, women and children as well as fabrics, notions and all kinds of dry goods. Obviously, they had prospered and it did my heart good.

I was introduced to the half dozen salespeople they employed. Immediately I was attracted to one of them, a very pretty girl who, I subsequently learned, was a school teacher acting as a salesgirl during her vacation. I lost no time in getting around to her for just the minute it took to whisper to her, "Where can I see you at eight tonight?" Without hesitation she told me, "At the ball park." I thought no one could possibly have guessed that in so brief a period I had made a date.

An hour or so later was store-closing time. My cousins

left me to spend a few days with my folks while they drove back to Drumright. They explained that they were eager to get back during daylight because the Ku Klux Klan held meetings at night at a point about half way between Shamrock and Drumright. They said it was not safe for Jews to be caught in such a spot because one could never know what "sport" hooded, masked men might indulge in, if by chance they ran into some Jews at night.

My folks lived in a frame shanty in the rear of the store. It was not surprising, because brick houses were a rarity in the oil regions. Most of the communities grew in an overnight boom in which settlers, a roving type, would hurriedly set up wooden dwellings.

The folks had a good cook and I remember enjoying all the meals prepared by Irene. At the dinner table we again talked about the Ku Klux Klan. I learned that business had fallen off considerably because the Klansmen and their families boycotted the store. To illustrate to what extent the K.K.K. was breeding hate, mistrust and disrupting friendships, my brother Abe told of how he was blackballed from the Masonic Lodge.

Prior to the K.K.K. operation, Abe was beloved by the community. He was a young man of about twenty-five, scrupulously fair in his dealings with everyone. He was exceptionally kind and openhanded in helping anyone who required it. With a population of less than fifteen hundred he was the town's idol, until the K.K.K. made the cross a symbol of hate. He was sadly disillusioned when he was denied admittance to membership in the Masonic Order. His bitter feeling was assuaged to some extent by the fact that in the still of the night some members of the Klan had expressed their sorrow. They vowed their unyielding affection for Abe but explained the necessity for their being members of the Klan.

A little before eight I told the folks I would like to roam about the town for a while. A little boy directed me to the park. I had no trouble in finding my date. She was as eager as I for the embrace, for the merging of warm breath as we paused between kisses to peer into each other's eyes and for the final fulfillment. I felt uneasy when the school Ma'am in the course of our later discussion about the K.K.K. revealed that her brother and father were members. She, however, appeared to be an intelligent, warm-hearted person who clearly understood the vicious place the Klan had assumed in American life. She thought that the Klansmen were generally irresponsible, shiftless men who failed as heads of families. She contrasted the unhappy, frustrated lives of most families in the community with the happy integrated lives of my people. She was farsighted and understood that the basis for the Klan's existence would be eliminated when the economy of our country was stable as well as prosperous. People who are well fed and well housed are not so apt to hate their neighbors as those who find the business of making a living a constant, unyielding torment.

The following night I prevailed upon my brother Abe to drive past the grounds where the Klan assembled. It was a gruesome sight. Cars filled with men were coming from both directions and parking on the big field opposite the Klan meeting place. Hundreds of men were already wearing their white hooded regalia, making a colorful sight as they moved about in the dark night with only the huge, lighted cross serving as a beacon. We had planned to drive through to Drumright, but on second thought considered it discreet to turn back.

Abe and I recalled the anti-Semitism we had experienced in our childhood at St. Louis. Because it emanated from Italians, Poles and Irishmen we felt it was strictly a Catholic phenomenon. Now, however, when we realized that the K.K.K. was strictly a Protestant organization, it made us think differently.

ISN'T IT FUNNY

## *Money Goes to Money?*

As I came into the coffee shop of the Huckins Hotel in Oklahoma City I saw Mr. Westheimer seated at the counter and was glad to grab the empty seat alongside of him. We ordered, chatted and finished our dinner. I had the fifteen cents ready to put down for my tip, but discretion prompted me to let the older and richer man make the first move. I saw him put down a thin dime and I followed his example.

That was back in 1922 when I was twenty years old and he was probably past sixty. He and his brother-in-law owned the big Westheimer and Daube store in Ardmore, Oklahoma. They also owned big oil fields and cattle ranches. They were easily the wealthiest family in their section of the country.

"Kid," Mr. Westheimer said to me, "I have about three hours to kill before catching the train to Ardmore. How about you and me hustling up a nice little poker game?" In a matter of minutes I made the rounds of the poolroom, coffee shop and lobby and returned with four other poor shnooks who, like myself, depended on our weekly check to eat and pay our hotel bills. We were called traveling salesmen.

When seated at the big table set up in Mr. Westheimer's room the question arose as to what limit we would play. All but our host took it for granted that it would be one dollar. The multi-millionaire, however, said that twenty-five cents was his top limit and reluctantly we proceeded.

When Mr. Westheimer looked at his watch a little past eleven P.M. he asked that we excuse him as he had to rush for his train. He won all the money and we were all practically broke. He made a cheerful get away and we were left to think and talk about the experience. Several of us had to wire our firms to send us money in order to continue on our trips. Had we played for higher stakes we would have really been in deep trouble.

We all agreed that as a rule rich men refuse to play for big stakes while those who cannot afford to lose are willing to risk their all. Too, it usually winds up that in a contest between the poor and the rich the latter is usually the winner.

So that old and trite as the expression is, it appears to be true that most often money goes to money.



## *Disappointed in Love*

Life as a traveling salesman was so rewarding to my sensual nature that I had little interest in my school work. That's why in my third year at Washington my work was poor, my grades were low and, finally, for the first time in my life, I flunked a subject. Having failed in college algebra, I decided to quit school, much to the disappointment of my relatives, who longed to have a college graduate in the family.

In the summer of 1923 I set out to travel on the road planning to make salesmanship a career. On this trip I decided to go straight across Missouri to Kansas City, winding up in Iowa. In Kansas City I was waiting for the buyer to finish with another young salesman. I stood by and watched. I was tremendously impressed. It seemed to me I could learn much from him. When he had completed his call I decided to follow him instead of seeing the buyer. As we came out on the street I approached him and introduced myself. His name was Al Greenfield, working for D. D. Greenfield, makers of children's dresses in New York City.

We met at the Baltimore Hotel that evening for dinner. We discovered we had something in common, rare among men traveling on the road. We both followed the Orthodox Jewish practice of praying every morning before breakfast in the traditional manner of putting on phylacteries. We did so on the Pullman trains or mezzanine floor of the hotel in the early hours of the morning. This drew us close together. We liked each other and compromises were made by both of us so that we could travel together for at least a few days. Though we were about the same age, he was a far more seasoned salesman, because he had been traveling consistently for the past few years. After a few days we wound up in Des Moines. He went north to Minneapolis while I continued east to Moline and then to Galesburg. I wanted to visit my sister and see the friends of my earlier youth.

I left Galesburg a fifteen-year-old boy, under five feet tall and weighing less than ninety pounds. Now I returned as a man of the world who had completed three years of college and as a traveling salesman. Everyone was amazed at the fact that I had shot up to normal height because they all thought I would be a midget. When I had left Galesburg, Hannah Michelson was a little girl of thirteen or fourteen, sweet and pretty, for whom I had the most tender feeling a boy of fifteen could possibly have. Now when I called at her home and saw her as a young lady of eighteen, I was smitten by her beauty and charm. She was attending Lombard College and was active in dramatic work. She was an extremely talented dancer and pianist. When we were children, Hannah's mother and my sister Sophie had often said in our presence, that some day Hannah would be my bride. Now, when I saw how lovely she had become I felt like staying in Galesburg to be near her. That is why I stopped there almost a week instead of the day or two I had planned. I spent every night with Hannah, going to the movie, having a soda, taking a walk or sitting at her home. Though I was far from being set in life, having no assured future, I was moved to such ecstasy that I proposed to her. She turned me down most graciously.

Though my proposal was made in utmost sincerity, it did not come about as a result of prolonged association with Hannah, but through the brief and sudden exposure to her exceptional qualities. For that reason my disappointment was not of long duration and left no emotional scars. For many years thereafter, I was keenly interested in anything I could learn about Hannah. To this day I have a soft spot in my heart for the girl who turned down my first proposal of marriage.

BOB BLACK

## *Illegitimate Business*

In the poolroom of the Hotel Tulsa I met Bob Black, who was selling for a Cleveland knit firm. I soon learned he wasn't doing well.

The few days I spent with Bob Black were memorable. He was one of the nicest fellows I ever met. His parents were both deaf mutes. Never exposed to harsh, irritant circumstances because of the extra compensatory love such marriages usually engender, Bob was either smiling or singing. There was, however, a melancholy note when he sang the sentimental ballads of the day, such as "Stories My Mother Told Me," "Little Rover, Rove All Over," and "There Are Smiles." When I thought of him in later years I analyzed him as being mildly frustrated because he hadn't succeeded in the career he cherished —acting. He wanted so badly to earn big money so he could be lavish in his treatment of the "love birds," as he called his parents. That explains why he was selling contraceptives to drug concerns as a sideline.

Bob revealed his predicament to me. There was a package at the express office containing about one hundred and fifty dollars worth of contraceptives rolled in casings and packaged as cigarettes. I phoned my boss, Mr. Goldberg, in St. Louis and told him the story. Sentimentalist that he was, he sent me an advance to help Bob get his money for passage to Dallas and for me to be set up in the contraceptive business.

A few hours after I had the supply of contraceptives delivered to my room, I had all the bellhops phoning and running up to buy packages for resale to guests in the hotel. I made several hundred per cent profit by this retail selling, but I was impatient to unload the entire stock. I had a guilty feeling about being in this business.

I was prompted to sell my entire stock to a wholesale drug concern at a nominal profit. This brief experience convinced me I was not cut out for any business that required selling in a "hush-hush" manner.

ROOM TO LET

## *Jews Not Wanted*

Returning from a long trip, I was persuaded by my family that road selling offered no future for me. We hit on a plan whereby I could return to college. This time I would study law.

My firm, National Skirt and Dress Company, agreed to give me a thirty dollar weekly drawing against commissions for sales after school hours. My school schedule was eight to noon. I chose the University of Chicago because that gave me a rich territory in the immediate vicinity of the school.

In the fall of 1923, when I was twenty, I enrolled at the University of Chicago Law School. I remember the day I matriculated, because it brought me into an acquaintanceship and a verbal clash with Nathan Leopold, who later committed one of the most sensational murders in the history of crime. While I was behind the doors of a lavatory in the men's room, I heard a discussion among a group of fellows with a single voice dominating the talk. This voice, strong and clear, in a brilliant argument took the position that college is no place for poor boys. He recognized the achievements of many poor boys who graduated from college but emphasized the fact that it was largely in the realm of the material. Few had made a real contribution to the cultural and spiritual advancement of the community. When one student mentioned Lincoln, the powerful voice said that Lincoln never went to college. He also countered with names like Washington, Jefferson and Hamilton to prove that aristocrats rather than men of the proletariat did most for their country.

Infuriated, I opened the door of the lavatory with a bang and rushed over to the circle of students as the magnetic voice was clinching his arguments. Without any apologies for intrusion, I injected myself into the discussion, telling them I was a poor boy who felt the right to go to college. I pointed my finger at the short, dapper Nathan Leopold and exclaimed, "Your insolence is an abomination unto the Lord."

The boys introduced themselves to me. I believe that among them were Maremont, Shainberg and Oberdorf. I know one of them was Lester Abelson, because it was he, whom I just met after twenty-two years, who reminded me word for word of the above quotation. In January, 1947, at the home of his sister, Mrs. England on San Marino Island, Miami Beach, I saw Lester for the first time since school days. We reminisced and I asked him whether he remembered my first contact with Leopold. "Do I?" said Lester. "I remember the very words you said to him!"

Nine months later Nathan Leopold, together with his partner in crime, Richard Loeb, were sentenced to serve life imprisonment for the kidnapping and murder of Bobby Franks, their thirteen-year-old neighbor.

The beauty and grandeur of the university overwhelmed me. It was situated near Washington Park and lovely Jackson Park. In this setting I looked for a place to live. The school dormitories were filled. The Housing Bureau of the University supplied me with a list of recognized boarding houses where I might obtain quarters. The closest address was the 6000 block on Ellis Avenue, which was directly across the Midway from the law school. In the first home I entered I was greeted by a charming, white-haired lady about seventy years old. She showed me to the only room she had available. It was small and had a studio couch. Spoiled by demanding only the best at first class hotels, in my previous years as a traveling man, I wanted a larger room and one with a bed. Politely I told the sweet lady it was the first stop and I was going to see a few other rooms. At the door, as I was about to leave, the gracious lady remarked, "I do wish you would come back to live with us. You are the kind my son and I would enjoy having. I could have rented the room to Jews but I wouldn't." With controlled emotions, this being my first encounter with the "restricted clientele" hostelry, I told her, "In that case you wouldn't want me, because I am a Jew." The poor old lady's cheeks flushed and she finally stammered, "Oh, I didn't mean one like you. You know what I mean. Now you would be welcome here." She went on to explain that her son was an associate professor at the school and that he disliked Jews for reasons she couldn't understand but that she went along with him in restricting her home. She felt it was a mistake and unchristianlike, but what could she do about it?

I discovered by questioning that on Sunday she and her son went to church services at Mandel Hall, the University Chapel. I then pointed out to her that in their most exalted mood she and her son prayed in a church which a Jew, Leon Mandel, donated to the University and prayed to Jesus who was of the Jewish faith. "Would you or your son refuse Jesus Christ or Leon Mandel a room because they were Jews?" I asked.

LOU GRUBER

# My Best Friend Is Gentile

Directly across the street from the "Christian" lady at 6024 Ellis Avenue, I met Mr. Nelson, who had two rooms available for students. He was a veteran of the First World War and a student at the university. A strikingly handsome man about thirty years old, he was married to an exquisite, petite redhead who nobly worked to help her husband complete his education. I told Nelson of the incident across the street. His wholesome comment was, "I'm a Protestant. One of my rooms is rented to a Catholic. Now if you take the other it will be a real demonstration of democracy." It was with a light heart that I rented the room from the Nelsons.

My landlord went on to describe Lou Gruber who had occupied the front room with the bay windows the previous semester. He was of German Catholic ancestry and lived in a small town in Indiana. Lou had taken his pre-legal work at Georgetown University. There he hobnobbed with the sons and daughters of senators and other interesting and influential families.

My room adjoined his and was separated by sliding doors. Nelson intimated that if Lou and I hit it off right we could use my room as a twin bedroom and convert Lou's room into a living room and studio. That's exactly what happened. In the first handshake and exchange of looks we knew we were meant to be friends. He arrived a day after I settled at 6024 Ellis Avenue and if one had witnessed our first night together at the dinner table at the Sixty-first Street "beanery," one would have surmised that we were inseparable buddies.

I was impressed by Lou's sophistication and etiquette,

by his impeccable attire and flawless manner of speaking. I considered it a privilege to have a society man take up with me, whose manners were those of a cloak-and-suit salesman. Where he was suave, I was unpolished. With his five-foot-nine, broad shoulders and one hundred and fifty pounds, I appeared anemic, weighing about one hundred and twenty-five pounds and standing five-foot-seven, in my shoes. When he slicked down his hair, which he parted in the middle, and finished his toilet, he looked as if he were the inspiration for the "Arrow collar" ad of the twenties.

Fortunately he was not a snob. In the many months of our Damon-Pythias relationship he never once criticized my many faulty habits. He genuinely liked my lisping speech and praised me no end because of my rigid adherence to orthodox Jewish rituals and prayers. I admired him equally for his genuine devotion to the faith of his inheritance. Often he attended Friday night synagogue services as my guest and by his ingratiating manner he succeeded in getting me to accompany him to Saturday night confession and early morning masses. Nurturing the bitter experience of my childhood, when Catholic boys violently attacked me and forced me to kiss the cross, I was grateful to Lou for awakening in me a spirit of tolerance and respect for his faith.

He was more mature than I in his thinking and aspirations. In a vague way I hoped to get a law degree and enter practice, whereas Lou had big dreams. Inspired by the shoe concern in Chicago operating under the name of O'Connor & Goldberg, he projected the name of Gruber & Goldfarb for a big law firm. He then planned to make politics a career and told me how effective our Catholic, Jewish combination could be. It was a cinch; he would get the Catholics and I would get the Jews. To Lou it was clear and real. To me it was merely an idea of a friend which called for a nodding of the head in approval and a word of encouragement. In any event, the team of Gruber & Goldfarb was recognized by most everyone at the law school.

MAN OF DISTINCTION AGREES

## *One Is Never Too Old to Learn*

Every lawyer knows that the greatest authority on the law of Agency is Mechem.

He was my professor at the University of Chicago in 1924. Then, in his middle seventies, he would appear in class with frock coat, gray striped trousers, wing collar, ascot tie and spats. He was tall and striking in appearance with his neatly trimmed beard and mustache.

The faculty in the law school were mostly men of distinction. We had Dean Hall, authority on torts. Hinton, noted on remedies and common law pleading, and the great authority on police power, Freund. Mechem, however, was regarded highest of all, as it was said that he alone, among all other American authorities on the law, was quoted in England's House of Lords.

One day in his class I raised my hand and when called on I said, "Professor, the principal could have received that information from the Credit Clearing House." Quickly he remarked, "I never heard of the Credit Clearing House." Now, like a reflex action, I shot back, "Well, one is never too old to learn."

The walls then shook with the raucous laughter of the more than one hundred students in the classroom. Only then did it occur to me that I must have pulled a faux pas in what I had said.

I spent a most uncomfortable time waiting for class to

end. Then from the rear of the room I started walking toward the professor's desk. Almost the entire class were behind me wanting to see what would transpire. I apologized to Professor Mechem. I told him I meant no disrespect by the remark I made and that I was sorry.

Then to the amazement of all the students he said, "Goldfarb, is the Credit Clearing House an organization similar to Dun and Bradstreet?" I answered in the affirmative. "Strange," continued Mechem, "I had never heard of them. Remember, Goldfarb, you need never apologize for telling the truth unless the telling of it would bring a hurt to the listener. No mature person should feel hurt when told 'one is never too old to learn'—nothing truer was ever said."

LOEB—LEOPOLD CASE

## *Witness to One of World's Greatest Tragedies*

In May 1924, the world-shaking Loeb-Leopold case made headlines. Imagine going to sleep peacefully one night and being awakened early in the morning by an ear-splitting "EXTRA, EXTRA! SOUTH SIDE COLLEGE BOYS KILL 13 YEAR OLD YOUTH." And then minutes later to hear the name of a classmate shouted. I heard the name Leopold again and again. I ran to my window and pulled it wide open and yelled out to the newsboy, "Did I hear you say Leopold?" "Yes," I was told. I urged the newsboy to rush from across the street—quickly got a coin from my pocket—I read the glaring headline confirming my wild instinctive suspicions. It was indeed none other than Nathan Leopold, the boy who sat near me in classes only yesterday—the boy who wrapped himself in my bathrobe in my room a few weeks earlier while studying with a group of us for exams—the boy whose father was a multimillionaire—the boy who told me he personally owned an office building, the boy who had two luxurious automobiles of his own—the boy who enthralled an audience with his lecture on the Kirkland Warbler, the boy who alone in a class of over one hundred could translate the Latin quotation for Dean Hall, the boy with whom I had a verbal clash on my first day at school—horribly, altogether too true, it was my classmate and his friend, Dickie Loeb who were accused of murdering thirteen-year-old Bobby Frank.

All three boys were sons of multi-millionaires. Leopold's father operated giant shipping lines on the Great Lakes. Loeb's father was vice-president of the great Sears, Roebuck and Company, and the victim's father, Mr. Frank, was president of the Illinois Watch Case Company.

All three boys were neighbors and friends. In fact Dickie Loeb was a cousin of the murdered child and even appeared as a pallbearer at the boy's funeral. The Frank's home was on the corner of Hyde Park Boulevard and Ellis Avenue. The Loeb home was directly across the street on Ellis Avenue, a house or two from the corner. Leopold lived a block or two away. The scene of the entire affair was only a few blocks from the university and exactly nine blocks from where I lived.

All three boys were Jews whose families were in the very top strata of Jewish society in Chicago. I feel certain their three families were members of the exclusive Standard Club to which in those days, only German and Spanish-Portuguese Jews of wealth and position were admitted.

Not long after the crime shocked the civilized world, all three fathers of the boys passed away.

First to die of a broken heart was Mr. Loeb, a refined,

cultured and able merchant who had been married to a woman of Catholic faith. The disgrace and humiliation were more than he could bear. Next to die was Bobby Frank's father, who was embittered because Loeb and Leopold escaped the death penalty. He left a sizeable sum in trust to be used at any future time if the killers sought to attain freedom from their life sentences in the penitentiary. Last to have death bring peace to a tortured soul was the widower Mr. Leopold. Undoubtedly he flagellated himself for substituting luxury and unbridled freedom for a mother's care for his motherless son, Nathan.

The crime received more newspaper publicity than any other up to that time. The Loeb-Leopold murder case was headlined in papers throughout the world. It was a crime that baffled not only the experts, but also the plain, ordinary citizens of all civilized countries who were seeking the answer to the simple question. Why? Why did they do it?

The facts, as I remember them were that Nathan Leopold and Richard Loeb, aged twenty and nineteen respectively, two brilliant graduates of the University of Michigan, doing postgraduate work at the University of Chicago, kidnapped for ten thousand dollars ransom, and later killed, thirteen-year-old Bobby Frank.

One afternoon the two murderers waited in Leopold's Willys Knight automobile near the private school which the victim attended. They had plans to kidnap some other child but any other child failing to come along, they spotted Bobby Frank and decided he would do just as well. Because the youth attempted an outcry when he sensed foul play, one of the murderers, probably Loeb, since Leopold was driving, picked up an iron bar and struck the blow which turned out to be fatal. While they may have intended merely to kidnap for ransom, they now found themselves murderers. They took the blood-stained body out to a desolate spot on the far south side. They then returned to Leopold's house and used the very typewriter he once brought to my room, to write the ransom note demanding ten thousand dollars from the slain boy's father for the "safe" return of the child. The ransom money was to be dropped from an elevated train somewhere on Sixty-third Street.

Bobby's parents followed to the letter the instructions contained in the ransom note. Loeb and Leopold appeared at school regularly without a day's absence all the while they perpetrated the nerve-shattering crime. The only way in which Leopold conducted himself differently in class from the time of the kidnapping to the time he was apprehended, a matter of several days—was that he sat in the rear all by himself. Only in retrospect, when the world knew of the crime, did we, his classmates, recall the peculiar fact that he did not sit in his customary place in the classroom.

Speculation ran rife among all at the University and particularly among us at the Law School, who were so close to Leopold. I barely knew Loeb because he was not in the Law School. I met him only once through an introduction from Leopold. Often, after the matter of their guilt became established, I wondered whether they might not have selected me as a victim for their wide range of crimes which was brought out at the trial. They were supposed to have committed castration on some poor taxi driver just for the sadistic thrill. I shuddered when I thought that because of Leopold's dislike and contempt for me, it might have been me instead of the taxi driver.

No doubt others in the Law School felt as I did. Whatever the case may be, there was little if any studying being done for the year-end examinations only a few weeks off. The excitement was at a very high pitch.

"Hanging bees" were being concocted daily all during the trial by numerous groups of law students in front of the school and library buildings. My thinking those days was on a level where I too felt the urge to join a mob to lynch our erstwhile campus mates and surely I was pulling for the death sentence.

The time we should have spent in studying for the exams was consumed instead in our following each word printed in the papers covering the case. As potential lawyers we followed the legal aspect of the case with scrupulous attention to all details.

It was only through a freak that the killing of Bobby Frank was positively traced to the real murderers. For days before Loeb and Leopold confessed to the commission of the crime, numerous suspects were apprehended and countless theories as to by whom and why the kidnapping was committed emanated from all sides. Then, by amazing chance, a man going to work one morning crossed the desolate spot where Bobby's body was almost completely encased in some huge drain pipe. Fortunately for justice, the worker spotted the bruised and bloody head of the child and notified the police. Detectives discovered a pair of eyeglasses near the victim's body. Clever search revealed the fact that the glasses were prescribed for Nathan Leopold by a State Street optical firm.

Events followed rapidly thereafter. Detectives learned from the Leopold's servants that Dickie Loeb was with Babe the day of Bobby Frank's disappearance from home. Having arrested both Loeb and Leopold, the police grilled them and got the weaker Loeb to admit the guilt of the crime through the trick of telling him that Leopold had already confessed, when in fact he had not. They pieced together enough facts in an alleged Leopold confession story to Loeb, and after considerable absence from Leopold, the two were brought face to face. By this time the pretty-faced, nineteen-year-old youth was so completely unnerved and worn as to denounce his erstwhile partner in crime as a rat for "spilling the beans."

Since I am reporting the story without reference to recorded files and solely from memory, I do not remember the prosecuting attorney. I believe it was Judge Caverly who presided. I know it was the world famous humanist and lawyer Clarence Darrow who defended the boys.

The world was left with the opinion that sex perversion was the chief factor that motivated the crime. Frankly, I do not remember what evidence was brought forth in this regard. At the time of the crime I, too, believed that sex perversion was the major reason.

After Loeb and Leopold were sentenced to life imprisonment I visited Leopold at the Joliet penitentiary as I shall tell in detail later on in the book. I was married and was calmer in considering the matter. I then concluded and still believe that the motive was simply that of seeking the thrill of committing the perfect crime. Those were the days of Al Capone and the greatest crime era in American history. Chicago was the heart and core of this orgy of murder and racketeering. Thrill-hungry Loeb and Leopold, in my opinion, wanted to prove that Capone and other notorious gang leaders were punks. To get the thrill of a lifetime they would commit the perfect crime. This, I believe was the sole motive for the kidnapping of Bobby Frank. If Babe Leopold reads this, I wish he would let me know whether I am right or wrong.

## GOLDFARB MANUFACTURING COMPANY

### *From Law School to Dressmaking*

I venture the opinion that the freshman class at the University of Chicago Law School in the exams of June 1924 had an overall average grade lower than any other class, unless the faculty graded them up in view of the extraordinary circumstances of the Loeb-Leopold case. Anyway, it gives me an alibi for flunking Real Property under Professor Bigelow, and making up my mind to quit college. Again my family was saddened by the fact that their youngest and most promising member would not honor them by getting a college diploma. To my knowledge, no member of our family on either my father's or mother's side had ever received a college degree.

By coincidence, on my return to St. Louis in July, I found my brother Morris withdrawing from his partnership in National Skirt and Dress Company which I had been representing. He approached me with a proposition to go into the dress manufacturing business with him. He would put up the entire capital of ten thousand dollars and give me one-third of the profits in addition to paying me a thirty dollar weekly salary plus all traveling expenses.

In a matter of weeks we opened in a small loft in an imposing garment building on Washington Avenue, under the name of Goldfarb Manufacturing Company. After Labor Day we were ready with our first line which consisted of a few solid color woolens and a few wool and cotton mixtures at three dollars and seventy-five cents per dress. I traveled east as far as Cleveland, making almost every city of seventy-five to one hundred thousand population. I didn't set the world on fire. I did a very quiet business, barely enough to cover my expenses. I had no conception of what I was selling as compared to what our competitors were offering. In those days I did not have an inquiring mind, eager to learn every phase of the enterprise that was occupying my time and energies. Nor did my brother know much about the dress business. In the few years he had been in it he did road selling so he had no opportunity to learn what in the trade is referred to as the "inside" of the business. Neither of us knew buying, styling or production. Nor had we ever been trained or taught to sell. We simply sold by the trial and error method of calling on customers, but without any preconceived plan. In this manner we muddled through.

JOLIET PENITENTIARY

## *A Surprise Visit with Leopold*

On August 7, 1925 I married Frances Young and settled in Chicago. Several weeks later on a trip to St. Louis we approached the giant penitentiary in Joliet, Illinois. Facetiously my wife remarked, "Your boy friend, Leopold, is in there, isn't he?" I immediately said, "Would you like to see him and spend some time with him?" Frances liked the idea. We drove over to the entrance gate of the high-walled prison. I asked the keeper whether we could visit Nathan Leopold. By coincidence it was visiting day, but our hopes were dampened when the guard told us he would announce us to Leopold but couldn't guarantee that he would want to see us. While waiting for his answer, I kept my fingers crossed; I would have wagered that the answer would be, "No," since no affection ever existed between us at school. To my amazement the answer came back that Nathan Leopold was on the prison farm, and was being escorted immediately to the visitors' hall to meet us.

The gates were opened and we were ushered into the prison grounds and then to the large room where the convicts met their guests. As I remember it, the room was about fifty to sixty feet long. One wall contained many tall windows. At both ends of the room there was a platform about eight or ten inches high, on which guards were seated with guns resting on tables in front of them. From one end of the room to the other, between the two raised platforms where the guards were seated, there was a long table about forty inches wide. On both sides of the table were ordinary straight benches without backs. As we entered the room there was a lone prisoner seated in the center of the long bench with his face to the windows, while two women sat directly opposite him. They were speaking in hushed tones and the eyes of the guards were glued upon them. The atmosphere of the room was tense which was to be expected when one found himself in a room which might harbor some of the Midwest's most noted criminals. We were seated but a minute or two when accompanied by a guard and breathing heavily as if he had been running, Nathan Leopold entered the room and exclaimed, "Hello, Goldy, how are you?" I was pleased to see how glad he was to see me. He sat down directly opposite us and I made the proper introductions. He expressed his best wishes for our happiness, and when he learned that Frances was from New York, he went on to tell of his interesting experiences on his visits there.

Presently a guard brought in a large basket filled with all kinds of fruit and a variety of cheeses, nuts and crackers. It was touching to witness that young man, heir to millions, nibbling away at the cheese and crackers, gulping down the food as if he had not partaken of any for a long time. He explained that it was a rare treat given to the prisoners only when they had visitors. I was amazed to discover that aside from his immediate family, we were the first visitors he had had in over a year. He asked what kind of car I was driving. I told him a poor man's car, a Chevrolet. In words that cast an air of poignancy in the room, he said, "I know you say that to be facetious—for you know that I'd give a million for the freedom that goes with the ownership of what you refer to as a poor man's car." He volunteered the information as to his future. "It's all behind me," he went on to say and indicated that if he were rated high for behavior, he could aspire in years to come to be placed on the prison farm for the rest of his life. In the meantime, he told us of his work, which consisted for the most part, in teaching his fellow prisoners.

The highlight of our interview with the most noted convict in America was his answer to my question about the ingenious tactics Clarence Darrow used to save them from the death penalty. We were astounded by Leopold's deprecation and denunciation of Clarence Darrow, then the foremost criminal lawyer in America. The whole world credited Darrow for doing the impossible, yet in blunt, plain words, Leopold said he wished he had been represented by Stewart and O'Brien. Leopold put in words like these, "True, if one wanted to get life imprisonment instead of death, Darrow was the right man; but if one wanted to get off scot free, Stewart and O'Brien were the better lawyers." He mentioned the fact that in the "Sheperd Case," Sheperd was acquitted despite conclusive evidence that he had used germs in food and medicine to bring slow death to the Pope boy, so that Sheperd could inherit the Pope millions. He credited Stewart and O'Brien with extra daring and though he admitted that his chance for acquittal was far less than Sheperd's, he felt Stewart and O'Brien would have done better than Darrow.

Before the visit came to an end Babe whispered to us that the fellow convict seated six or eight feet away from him was some "killer" or other. Then we saw "killer" who probably rose from shantytown to become a gangster king, walk out of the visiting room together with Babe Leopold, heir to millions and dazzlingly brilliant. The "killer" put his arm about Leopold's shoulder and under the watchful eye of the guard behind him, the two convicts left the room as though they were the closest pals.

CHICAGO

## *Babies, Prosperity and Adversity*

When I married I became associated with a children's dress firm by the name of D. D. Greenfield. I was given a year's contract that called for my selling their line in Missouri, Iowa and Illinois. I was to receive $100.00 weekly. After paying traveling expenses it left me about $40.00 a week.

In July 1926 I became a proud father. Barely 15 months later baby number two arrived. The first was named Gene and the second was named Murray.

In 1927 I severed my connection with Greenfield and the children's dress business. I connected with Cornbleet Brothers, a St. Louis manufacturer of housedresses, who paid me 7% commission on sales. I also took on a side line of cotton dresses from Maidwell Garment Company, Forrest City, Arkansas.

I no longer had to travel as my territory was Chicago

and the surrounding fifty-mile area. I could be home nightly and had no traveling expenses, but best of all I was with my family. It was my pleasure each night after dinner to go to the bathtub and on my knees wash the day's accumulation of diapers from my two babies.

In 1927 my income skyrocketed from $2,000 to $7,000 a year. In 1928 it jumped to $13,000.

Despite a soaring stock market I managed to find the stocks that lost practically every dollar I invested in them. Then Mr. Cornbleet sought to make other arrangements with me which were unsatisfactory. Happily I phoned Mr. Ed Ash in Arkansas. I told him of my severing with Cornbleet and my desire to move to New York City. Though I handled his line for two years I had never met him and was delighted when he said he would reimburse me for the expenses in coming down to see him.

I was the only passenger to alight from the train so Mr. Ash had no trouble in recognizing me. He was surprised at my being so young. From my correspondence he had judged me to be an older man.

Mr. Ash told me his New York representative wasn't doing well and that he would be happy to have me represent him. Unfortunately he was a small operator with a limited capital. I doubt whether he had even $20,000.00. The deal was for me to get a straight 7% commission on sales, but he advanced me $500 to help me move East and have a few weeks' pay.

It was with a heavy heart that I made the move to New York City. Frances was pleased with the thought of being close to her family, but financially we never dreamed that I would ever do as well again as I had done in Chicago.

NEW YORK

## *Yokel Boy Makes Good*

In the middle of February 1929, my family and I burned our bridges behind us and moved to New York. We rented a four room apartment on Eastburn Avenue in the Bronx.

My business, however, was launched the first day after our arrival. I was prepared to show an item in which I put my faith, to get me started successfully in the East. I had Mr. Ash make a wraparound garment in a material that had probably never before been used for women's utility garments. It was a cheap, solid-color organdy. It was used for curtains and as trimming for ladies' house-dresses. Ed Ash started to cut one hundred dozen before I left Arkansas so that they would be ready for shipment when I sent in my orders.

On my second day in New York fate directed me to call on Mr. Clarence Goss, the buyer for W. T. Grant Company. I walked out of his office with a trial order for thirty dozen, which, in his presence, I named "Servicettes." Three dozen each were ordered for ten of the largest stores in the deep South, where sheer summery garments were selling far earlier than in the North. I remember the location of some of the stores to have been in Tampa, Jacksonville, Fort Worth and Houston. Within an hour the order was long-distanced to Arkansas, and Ed Ash assured me the dresses would be rushed out to the Grant stores that very day. Before a week passed I had a call from Mr. Goss telling me of the large re-orders he had already received. He placed a distribution order with me for all the Grant stores amounting to over one thousand dozen.

Ed Ash gambled on his judgment in staking me. Now he gambled his last dollar in expanding to take care of big business. I succeeded in placing the item with other chains and by the middle of April we were swamped with re-orders. Ed continually added machines. By May it became evident that Maidwell could not fill half the re-orders from the chain stores, so I sent a telegram to about ten large midwestern manufacturers telling them I could get them all the business they could handle on one garment if they assured me of deliveries. By May fifteenth I was representing three other firms—all making the "Servicette" but in different materials and slight variations in styling. One of the firms was Rhea Manufacturing Company of Milwaukee. Today Rhea is one of the large manufacturers of Junior sportswear in America.

In June 1929 I made more money than I had ever made previously in my life. I then knew I had no reason to fear New York City, and could always make a living if I had my health. Chiefly because I couldn't stand riding the subways, coupled by my dislike for the congestion in the Bronx, we took a two bedroom efficiency apartment in Long Beach, Long Island, with the idea of spending the summer there. To me it was a virtual paradise. I loved its clean, wide streets in contrast to the dirty, narrow ones in the Bronx. It was primarily a community of private homes, mostly of brick and stucco construction, all with red tile roofs—as required by an ordinance of the town. It made a pretty sight. The air was always crisp and fresh, and above all, I enjoyed the sight and the sound of the ocean. I thrilled to the roar of the waves and the never-ending spectacle of the white caps. It was in Long Beach that I had my first view of an ocean and I was captivated by it. The first summer there was a glorious climax to my successful business conquest of America's largest city.

## EASY COME, EASY GO

### *The Greatest Stock Market Crash*

All of 1929, while I enjoyed my newly found success in New York, the stock market was boiling. Prices advanced so high that many of the foremost economists said that the United States had reached a position where the people would enjoy prosperity on a scale hitherto undreamed of. President Hoover said, "From now on the American people could expect two chickens in every pot." Under the circumstances, the big commission checks I had been receiving weighed heavily in my pockets. Besides, the nature of my business had changed radically.

In Chicago I had to call on buyers from store to store all day long. In New York, once the styles were adopted and sold successfully by the chain stores, I had nothing to do but sit back and collect commission checks. The hardest job I had each day was the pleasant one of opening my morning mail and totalling the shipments my companies had made for me the previous day. Each morning at nine fifteen I figured how much money yesterday's shipping at the factory meant for me on my month-end commission statement. One thousand dollar shipments meant seventy dollars, two thousand dollar shipments meant one hundred and forty dollars. It was an exhilarating experience to look forward to each day. I have an idea that the tearing open of those envelopes gave me a feeling not too unlike that of the big capitalist who enjoys clipping the coupons of his bonds and other securities.

My living expenses were low. My apartment rental at a seaside resort town was only nine hundred dollars for the full year. I was never clothes conscious. I was wearing forty dollar suits and continued to do so even in later years when I earned one hundred thousand dollars a year. Out in the country on week-ends, my greatest pleasure was to push the carriage with my two beautiful baby boys.

I could have saved a lot of money but I didn't. Money easily earned is generally easily spent. I squandered it. I went back into the stock market about mid-June and lost every dollar I invested.

Here is a sample of my daily routine after reaching my office. First, I figured my previous day's shipments at the factories. Next, I might pick up the 'phone and call a few buyers to try to get them to come to the office. About nine forty-five I would rush down from the tenth floor to the second floor where the stock brokerage firm of Coombe, Kerr and Pratt was located. That gave me fifteen minutes before the market opened to look over what are called "dope" sheets. Various firms issue daily bulletins predicting what may happen in the market generally, and to certain securities, in particular. In later years I wondered whether they call them dope sheets because the people who take them seriously are "dopes."

From ten o'clock to three o'clock in the afternoon, when the market closes, I spent every minute of my time watching the ticker and exchanging ideas with the large number of other steady suckers who crowded the room. I gave myself about fifteen minutes for a standing lunch at the counter downstairs in the Exchange Buffet, and often passed up lunch if the ticker conveyed some exciting quotations. Occasionally, I would go into the booth and phone my secretary to find out what was happening, but more often I would wait for her to call me. She called only when some important buyer appeared. I spent more time as a trader in the brokerage office than I did in taking care of my business. However, I did not fail Mr. Ash in getting all the business he could handle.

I never was a good trader, and though I made a few good buys which brought me profits, I always wound up losing. To this day I can say that in my lifetime I have never ended up making a dollar in any investment. I have always made money in the business I understood and in which I became professional, but every time I tried making money in a venture where the other fellow was professional and I a mere amateur, I lost all but my proverbial shirt.

I was a witness to the greatest stock market crash in the history of our country. The first break came in September. It took everyone by surprise. It was as if someone had been thrown to the ground without seeing what had struck them. We in the brokerage office were hit hard but didn't know how to account for it. We were given no warning. In a vague way I remember the tension on the faces of my companions at the brokerage office exhibited each day from the time the crash came until that dark, miserable day in October that has gone down in history as Black Friday. I honestly think the day was a really dark one outside. It was the most memorable one I shall ever recall, insofar as I was a witness to people breaking down in grief and actual tears, as they read the ticker tape and saw the value of their securities dwindle to losses which left most of them broke. The Thursday session of the stock exchange was bad enough. At ten o'clock the following morning of Black Friday, there was no standing room in the Coombe, Kerr and Pratt's office and I imagine that was the scene throughout the country. People waited with tantalizing anticipation to see how the market would open when the ten o'clock gong sounded. I don't believe there was a light heart in that brokerage office. The minute that preceded ten o'clock of Black Friday was as tense and dramatic a moment as I shall probably ever again experience. I feel certain there was not a smile on the face of any of the several hundred men and women who were awaiting the Sword of Damocles which the ticker tapes of America represented for stockholders on that fateful day.

No one expected a good opening. Yet I do not believe one person in a thousand anticipated the awful crash in prices that occurred. From the first recorded transaction that the ten o'clock tape revealed until late that night, when the "many hours late" ticker told a story to rock the universe, stocks were sold in quantities and at prices no person had ever thought possible. One block after another came out in ten thousand, twenty thousand and I believe even fifty thousand shares at prices from ten dollars to thirty dollars less than the previous night's closing. To give you an idea of the shock and surprise to which we were all exposed, consider the fact that White Sewing Machine went from fifteen to one dollar at the end of the day. Several women and one man I knew intimately fainted as the particular stock they owned came out on the ticker and transmitted the heartbreaking fact that their margin account was wiped out. All through that memorable day one kept hearing from the stunned watchers of the ticker, that they were cleaned out.

For millions of people the crash in the stock market meant a change in their mode of living. Many had the feeling of being wealthy or at least well off, only to realize that paper profits in Wall Street can evaporate. Accustomed to a nominal living standard and having continuity of good earnings, I hardly missed the thousands of dollars I lost. Steady, large earnings made possible new savings. Like many other amateurs I felt the crash on Black Friday meant that stocks had reached bottom and it was, therefore, safe to buy again.

Acting on this theory, I foolishly bought stocks every time I accumulated a few thousand dollars and lost my money with regularity each year.

DAVID'S DEATH

## *I Begin to Think for Myself*

The death of David, my sister Lottie's twenty-one year-old son, was the greatest tragedy our family had experienced to date. He was a lovable person for whom I had great affection.

I was badly shaken and grieved for months thereafter. I began to question the way of the Lord. Why should one so young, innocent and kind be taken and others leading parasitical and evil lives be given length of years?

I wondered what sense it made for me to observe daily the orthodox Jewish practice of wearing the phylacteries at prayer each morning. I began to think and question everything. Why God? Why Judaism? Why life? Why death? Why disease? Why poverty? Why riches? Why crime, why graft, why war and peace?

All my life I attended the High Holy Day services on the Jewish New Year praying devoutly. Now as a young father at thirty I spent the day questioning. I studied the faces of those engaged in prayer. I wondered how many took seriously what they were saying. What change would it make in their lives? How would it manifest itself in their behavior back on their jobs?

I was especially perturbed by the realization that four years of college taught me so little. There were no books in my house and I never read the editorial page of a newspaper. All I read were the headlines, the stock market news, the sport pages and the comic sheets. It dawned on me that I was existing, but not actually living. I ate, slept, worked and played, but did nothing to improve myself as a person.

In that frame of mind I passed a newsstand and saw a title on a magazine that intrigued me. "What I Believe," by Everett Dean Martin. For the first time in my life I bought a serious piece of literature as I placed fifteen cents on the counter and walked away the proud possessor of *The Nation* magazine.

That night I must have read the article half a dozen times. Try as I might I could not find a paragraph, phrase or single word with which I could disagree. What Mr. Martin believed I too believed. I strongly recommend to my readers that they buy a reprint of Mr. Martin's article in the October 21, 1931 issue of *The Nation.*

Here are some excerpts together with my comments on the right hand side:

> *"What we believe is unimportant but to the Educator how and why we believe is* more *important."*

*Read this over. Read this twice. Read it until you understand that it applies to you and that you resolve to challenge every belief you hold.*

> *"Most of our beliefs have been acquired irrationally; they have been fostered in us during childhood; they are accepted on authority, they are the result of asserting that things are so merely because we want them to be so; they are often based on prejudice and tribal legend and are maintained as face saving devices."*

> *"I do not see why a man's convictions should be respected unless he has made an honest, coura-*

*Have you?*

*geous effort to ascertain the truth of them."*

*"In my own belief I can find no hypothesis which it is conceivable I should be unwilling to modify or discard."*

*Can you say the same?*

*"I prize knowledge because it makes a difference between men and animals and between higher men and lower."*

*Never, but never forget this.*

*"Our evangelical Protestantism with its repeated emphasis on 'Change of Heart' has emphasized right feeling at the expense of right thinking."*

*Isn't this true about all orthodox religions?*

*"Now I suspect that the mess this world is in at the present time is largely the result of the precedence of the salesman over the man of thought. A world dominated by sales mentality must necessarily be cheap and tawdry, negligent of finer values and remote ends. It must proceed by pandering to the mob, it must be led by men of second rate minds. I cannot say that such a way of life inspires in me any profound belief."*

*Considering this was written in 1931, don't you believe that Mr. Martin prophesied Mussolini and Hitler and the world they helped to create in the 1940's?*

*"I PREFER THE SINCERE TO THE SUCCESSFUL PERSON. THAT IS, I BELIEVE IN A KIND OF SPIRITUAL INTEGRITY*

*Remember this every time you compare a*

*NOT EASILY TURNED TO PROFIT IN THIS COMMERCIAL AGE."*

*poor Einstein with a rich Thyssen.*

*"I believe that what people become is more to be considered than what they can get."*

*"In a world of advertising and salesmanship the technique of saying and doing things for effect is so important, and the financial reward for manipulating the public by appealing to its vanity is so great, that our people have developed the fixed habit of systematory and persistent self-deception. HE WHO KNOWINGLY DECEIVES OTHERS IS DISHONEST, HE WHO DECEIVES HIMSELF IS INSINCERE."*

*PLEASE TRY TO UNDERSTAND THIS.*

*"I prefer the mentally mature to those who are content to enter the Kingdom of Heaven as little children. I cannot agree to the proposition that it is necessary to keep all mankind in perpetual infancy in order to protect them from temptation or save their souls."*

*This is a true criticism of all orthodox creeds and those who believe in them.*

*"Perhaps in some future we may be wise enough greatly to improve our human lot. BUT WE MUST FIRST CREATE SOMETHING IN AND OUT OF OUR-*

*This hit me!*

*SELVES. AND NOT UNTIL WE GROW UP SHALL WE KNOW WHAT REALLY TO DESIRE."*

That night it took me much longer to fall asleep than any other. I tossed in my bed for hours pondering the many ideas in Mr. Martin's article which shook me out of my mental lethargy and made me realize that I was not a thinking person. I realized that I was a slave to ritual, dogma, ways of living handed down to me and accepted in blind faith but which I had never tried to figure for myself. In the early hours of the morning I concluded that I would never fall asleep that night until I resolved the conflict raging in my heart and mind. Was I going to continue living as I did, as most people do, or was I going to grow up and become mentally and spiritually a man rather than an adolescent? "What I Believe" made me realize I could feel, but that I was unable to think, and much less able to express myself. More than ever I deprecated the value of the four years I had spent in college. I became infuriated when I considered that my college training had still left me an unthinking, uneducated person. Mr. Martin's article hit the bull's eye, as far as I was concerned. I fell asleep only after my resolve to expose myself to every avenue that led to the improvement of my mind. I resolved to begin reading on the subjects that I was interested in, and about which I wanted to form objective conclusions. I resolved to expose myself to people from whom I could learn in order to broaden my outlook. I made up my mind to challenge every thought, every act I was accustomed to, and change to a different course, if it failed to meet the best of my reasoning ability.

I awoke the following morning cognizant of the fact that a metamorphosis had taken place in my being. In the words of Coleridge's *Ancient Mariner,* "A sadder but a wiser man he rose the morrow morn." I must have been subdued that morning when for the first time since my Bar Mitzvah ceremony at the age of twelve, I failed to put on my phylacteries, but simply said a prayer of my own choosing.

In my office I began to look upon people in a way I had never done before. I would ask myself whether a person was a thinking individual as I felt I was on the road to becoming, or simply existed as I had been doing all of my life.

Maurice Oppenheimer, of the textile house of Brand and Oppenheimer, called on me. His polished manner denoted a man of culture and learning. He stood out from the rest of the salesmen whom I knew. I cultivated him and found my impressions to be sound. I learned he was a college graduate, which was a rarity among textile or garment salesmen in those days. He was extremely well read and interested in everything worthwhile, including good music. Three or four times a week we lunched together.

A new world unfolded itself to me at these luncheons. Instead of talking wine, women and song, or confining ourselves to talking business, as most people do, we discussed religion, politics, economics, and interesting books and people. Here it was that I was initiated into the habit of buying good books, which resulted in my accumulating a library of several thousand volumes over the years. The first important book I read was *Lincoln Steffen's Autobiography*. I thoroughly enjoyed it. To this day I quote from it. I recommended it as a "must" to my friends, including my sons, when they started on the road of self-education through good reading and conversing. Soon thereafter I read Bertrand Russell's *Conquest of Happiness*, which I have recently reread and found as stimulating and exhilarating as when I read it the first time. None of the books I have ever read offers the reader so lucidly and simply wise guidance and direction for sane healthy living as does the *Conquest of Happiness.* It's a pity that our schools and colleges often fill the minds of their students with all kinds of balderdash. Dozens of books are made required reading which leave the student with little if anything at all to make life better and easier to understand. On the other hand, a book such as *Conquest of Happiness* if thoroughly studied and indelibly impressed on a student's mind, is certain to make a vital contribution to his growth as a human being.

## INSULT SELLING

### *Sometimes a Necessity*

As a salesman for Maidwell I made several unsuccessful efforts to sell the great firm with headquarters in Detroit . . . the S. S. Kresge Company. Not once could I get to see the buyer. Either he was in conference, all bought up or gave me some other excuse.

On this particular trip in 1932 I was taking note of the grandeur of the building and grounds, the magnificent pictures hanging on the walls in the lobby and the splendor of the office building. They even had a midget that could be taken for a duplicate of the one noted for his clear, resounding, "Call for Philip Morris," to take one's business card to the buyer.

The boy returned saying that Mr. Secord could not see me. I went to the nearest phone booth, asked for Mr. Secord's secretary and told her I had just made a special trip from Forrest City, Arkansas and felt entitled to a five minute interview, having never been given a chance to meet her boss. I waited a moment and was told to return to their building. The "Philip Morris" boy in full regalia escorted me down the spacious aisle to a door where a man stood straddling the doorway leading from the hall into a spacious sample room. "All right, young man, I'm going to give you the five minutes you asked for," said the gentleman.

I protested and said that I could not believe Mr. Kresge invested a fortune in the most beautiful offices I had ever seen in my life if he didn't intend to convey hospitality to those who came to call on their buyers. I wanted five minutes seated in a chair in Mr. Secord's private office.

Reluctantly I was granted my request and as the buyer sat down in his chair he removed his wrist watch and placing it on his desk said, "Okay, you have my attention for five minutes."

I said, "Mr. Secord, I took a walk down Woodward Avenue last night to shop the windows. Practically every store had a display of cotton dresses, but if I had to award a booby prize for the poorest display in town I would give it to your store."

The buyer, with reddened face, asked me if I had come all the way from Arkansas to insult him. I explained that I was not condemning the merchandise on display, but rather the shabby manner in which it was presented to the public. I told him I estimated the window dresser threw in at random over thirty to forty garments, all wrinkled instead of showing five to eight garments neatly pressed and draped, with a suitable sign to let the people know what was useful or special about the merchandise.

When Mr. Secord was convinced that I was not knocking his style or quality selection he asked whether I would repeat my suggestions to a gentleman in charge of display that he was taking me to meet. While walking I told him if he did business with me the service went beyond my getting the order . . . that I would cooperate with display and promotional ideas. Five minutes turned into almost a half hour and I left a smiling Mr. Secord with an opening order for six hundred dozen dresses.

Thirty years have passed and I am happy to state we still enjoy doing business with the Kresge Company.

LUST FOR LEARNING

## *Exposure to Broadening Influences*

Reading books, conversing and exchanging ideas with good friends, whetted my appetite for other means to help me learn "what it was all about." I hung on every word of Father Coughlin's tirades against big business and Wall Street bankers. This was in 1932 when he had not yet desecrated his holy garb by preaching hate and poisonous propaganda which ultimately led to his forced withdrawal from the air. In Forest Hills, where we had moved from Long Beach, we were regular attendants of the Friday Evening Services by Rabbi Sol Landman.

I am grateful to him for many enlightening sermons. One in particular has served as a basic pillar in my thought and action, ever since I heard it. The sermon dealt with the Jewish sage, Hillel, who said, "If I am not for myself, who will be for me? If, however, I think only of myself, what am I?" Here I sensed was a formula for living, easy to remember, understand and follow. Since my sons were old enough to speak whole sentences I have endeavored to impress them with the wisdom of living by Hillel's admonition.

On Sundays I went to the Community Church at Town Hall in New York, where Dr. John Haynes Holmes spoke with eloquence seldom matched by any preacher in our time. That church did more to initiate me into genuine tolerance and understanding than any other institution which I had ever attended. Here one would sit in an audience composed of all kinds of people. There were white, black and yellow skinned. Catholics were not likely to be present in large numbers, but every denomination of Protestants, large numbers of Jews, Mohammedans, Buddhists, and even atheists were banded together in fellowship. It was thrilling to come into a church where a Negro or Chinese might lead you to your seat, and you might find yourself seated next to a Hindu or Turk. Here was democracy at its best. Frequently the church would have Sunday night community dinners. I attended several and I was thrilled to be with people of all races and creeds at a dinner that could truly be termed a spiritual feast. At one of these dinners we were charmed by a Hindu at our table who made us realize that no nationality, no religion or race had a monopoly on culture or wisdom. We learned that all peoples have much to learn from one another, that together we are a beautiful integrated whole, while apart, we tend to become predatory savages who would eventually destroy one another. Here at the Community Church was a demonstration that all people could unite as one, in worshipping truth and The One God, Common Father to all mankind.

Occasionally Dr. Holmes exchanged pulpits with other liberal preachers or lay leaders. Once I heard Professor William Lyons Phelps, revered and beloved at Yale for decades. The important point he developed in his talk was that we are alive only to the extent that we are interested. The more interested the more alive. If, for instance, one has no interest in baseball it means one is dead insofar as baseball is concerned. The same applies to music, books, dancing, food, gardening, politics and every other phase of human activity. Dr. Phelps made it clear that one could not be interested in everything, but suggested that everyone try to interest himself in as many of the better and important facets of human activity as possible.

In addition to the regular Sunday sermons at Community Church, one could buy for only ten cents a copy of many sermons which were preached in previous years and which were in printed form. I bought them all. I don't remember listening to or reading any sermon delivered by a liberal preacher which has failed to teach me. On the whole I believe I have received better instruction and guidance for good living from sermons than from any other medium of education. I strongly recommend to my readers that they cultivate an appreciation for sermons emanating from liberal preachers. Clergymen representing fundamentalist denominations in Protestantism, Orthodox Judaism or Roman Catholicism seldom present what I would consider universal truths in their sermons. Their respective faith is predicated on too narrow and dogmatic a belief that they alone are God's favored children. If ever there is to be a realization of one people, living in brotherhood in one world, worshipping one God, it can only come about by liberal thinking and believing souls, who accept the sane, moderate view of the Hebrew prophet, Malachi who proclaimed, "Have we not all one Father? Hath not one God created us?"

My quest for learning continued each day. For instance, in mid 1932, when the depression was at its worst, I visited Mr. Ash, my employer at Forrest City, Arkansas. One evening I found myself surrounded by eight teenagers. They were drawn to the sophisticated New Yorker they considered me to be. They plied me with many questions about Broadway, the theater, the orchestra leaders, the style of dancing, the standing of the baseball teams. I was struck by the fact that these fine, bright youngsters showed no interest in the tremendous, awful problems of our country or the whole world. There were dark clouds overhanging the universe. People were struggling and starving by the tens of millions. Hitler was emerging in Europe and making it clear that he was out to destroy the spiritual and ethical values by which decent people lived everywhere. In America, Franklin Delano Roosevelt was offering hope to the Americans and also to the peoples of the entire world by his dramatic presentation of a New Deal for the common man. Yet here in Forrest City, Arkansas, these bright high school youngsters were showing an interest only in the meaningless things of life. To test their attitude, I put this question to them: "If tomorrow a train on which President Herbert Hoover and Babe Ruth were passengers, stopped for a few minutes at the railroad station and you had time to see only one of them, whom would you want to see?" Their unanimous answer was that they would want to see Babe Ruth. In fact, they implied I must be joking to infer that the question presented a serious choice.

Now, I am not intimating that these Arkansas youngsters registered the attitude of all American children. I do believe, however, that it did represent the feeling of a large majority of them. I can't help feeling that the apathy in matters spiritual, economic, and political which these children revealed had a direct relationship to our becoming involved in World War II.

About thirty years later I visited Russia. What impressed me more than their scientific marvels was the discovery that children below the teenage level were already reading the editorial page of the newspapers. It is a fact that Communist children receive a better education than ours. For that reason Admiral Rickover is presently pleading that we improve our educational standards.

DALE CARNEGIE

## *He Taught Me to Think on My Feet*

Forum meetings at the Forest Hills Jewish Center gave added delight to living in that beautiful surburban community. Each week during the fall and winter seasons, a prominent speaker would deliver an address which was open to all. The question and answer period was always stimulating and because of my eagerness for knowledge, I asked at least one question at every meeting. I was extremely nervous whenever I got on my feet to ask a question. My friends noticed that my legs actually trembled, as did my voice, whenever I got up to express myself. I was self-conscious, and aware of the fact that my knowledge on any subject was inadequate. That accounted for my inability to speak on my feet or even to ask a simple question. It was therefore with eagerness that I accepted an invitation one evening to join Hal Lebosky, a buyer for the firm of Felix Lillienthal, to attend a course in public speaking given by a relatively unknown named Dale Carnegie. This was in the fall of 1933. Several years later Dale Carnegie's book *"How to Win Friends and Influence People"* became the best-selling non-fiction book ever published.

That evening I dined with Hal Lebosky and a number of his friends and business associates. I learned that Mr. Lillienthal and his partner, Mr. Greenebaum, were taking the course and invited all of their executives to join them. After dinner I went along with the men to a meeting room at the Advertising Club on Park Avenue. There were about forty people in the class. Mr. Carnegie conducted the course. The session started off with a bang. After a brief minute or two of introductory remarks, Mr. Carnegie called on each person in the room to come to the front and speak for one minute on any subject. It was most amusing to witness grown men, successful in business or profession, unable to speak coherently, and faltering at almost every word spoken. It made me feel good to discover that almost everyone found it as difficult as I did to get up and address a group.

After the fourth or fifth person finished, I passed a note to Mr. Carnegie telling him my name and asking him to consider me a member of the class as of that evening. In less than a minute, the student who was speaking concluded and the very next one to be called by Mr. Carnegie to speak was "Sam Goldfarb." I dragged my feet forward as if they were lead. I stumbled and mumbled but could get no words to emanate from my mouth. I was semi-paralyzed with fright. I felt as if I were going to collapse. I said something about being totally unprepared, and was making ready to drag my nerve-exhausted body back to my seat, when Mr. Carnegie, sensing my plight said, "Sam Goldfarb, tell me where you live, about your family, about your business—anything at all which no one knows as much about as you do." I managed to utter a few half intelligent sentences and returned to my seat a nervous wreck.

When the course was over, thirteen weeks later, Dale Carnegie called at my office and appealed to me to speak on his behalf before an expected audience of twelve hundred people at the Advertising Club auditorium. Though I had made wonderful progress during the weeks of diligent effort in the course, I nevertheless felt unable to speak before total strangers, and especially before so large a group. It is one thing to speak to a small group, all of whom are known to one; it's another matter to speak to an unknown audience. Truly I was afraid to do it but I yielded to Mr. Carnegie's persuasion. As I remember it, there were three speakers besides Mr. Carnegie. One I can't recall, one was Lowell Thomas and I was the third! The gist of my talk was to describe how I was unable even to ask a question at a forum meeting, and how the Dale Carnegie Course made it possible for me to stand before them and express myself. I wound up predicting that my income which was at the rate of about fifteen thousand gross for the year would within ten years reach over fifty thousand dollars. My prediction was more than fulfilled, for ten years later I was earning over one hundred thousand dollars a year.

THE PRIZE WINNING SPEECH

## *I Tell the Truth about Myself*

The directors of the Dale Carnegie Course of Public Speaking give a prize at each session to the one whose one minute speech is voted best by the members of the class.

Back in 1933 when Mr. Carnegie was conducting the classes himself and before he gained international prominence I won a prize for this speech:

"Ladies and gentlemen, before you stands a mediocre man. I swear a little, lie a little, I envy, I hate, I drink, I smoke, and I gamble. I have stolen in my adolescence and along the way I have cheated, faked, and misrepresented. In fact, you name the vice and I have in my time probably been guilty of committing it.

I console myself because I have never knowingly hurt

another. Moreover, I am heartened by the fact that each year as I grow older I also grow up. When I take inventory I find my stock of good constantly increasing and my stock of bad diminishing. Each year I get to like myself a little more."

MY LAST JOB

## *The End of My Sales Career*

About ten weeks after appearing as a speaker in behalf of Dale Carnegie and predicting a rosy future for myself, I was out of a job. Mr. Ash, head of Maidwell Garment Company, decided to liquidate the company rather than operate under the newly-organized National Recovery Act.

Fortunately I had not lost all my money in the stock market. With about ten thousand dollars in the bank the wolf was not even close to our door. It was nevertheless a stunning blow to now be out of a job when I was known to be one of the biggest money makers in our industry.

At that critical time I received a visit from Mr. John Poland of Perfection Garment Co., Martinsburg, West Virginia. He had heard of Maidwell's decision to quit and came to offer me a job.

I eagerly accepted his two hundred dollar a week offer to manage the New York office and moved to 1350 Broadway on January 2, 1934.

Mrs. Rose Merkle was my secretary and assistant. She had a million-dollar personality and was beloved by everyone. Even with her capable assistance I failed to do a good job. While Perfection's quality was tops, the patterns used and the styling of the dresses were weak.

The passing of each week was very trying for me. It

was not that conditions were unpleasant; quite the contrary, they were altogether too pleasant. For the first time in my life I was surrounded by luxury. Our offices were matched by few in that twenty-five story building. Previously I had never known what it was to have a private office of my own. The whole atmosphere enhanced by the sweet personality of Rose should have made me happy, but instead I was morose. It was a painful experience to open the factory mail and see my weekly pay check. Bear in mind that when income tax and cost of living are considered, the two hundred dollars of 1934 was at least as good as one thousand dollars in 1964. I felt I was not earning the money. Though I had been accustomed to earning more, the former earnings were commissions for orders I procured. Now I was on a straight salary and I realized that if I were on a commission basis I should be earning about half of what I was getting.

For this reason I wrote Mr. Poland telling him I was ready to release him from his contract for the remaining six months of the year. He replied that in thirty years' business experience no salesman had ever offered to make him a present of monies which the salesman could legally continue to collect. At Mr. Poland's request I stayed until August first, when for the last time in my life I drew compensation as an employee. For though I had no idea—none whatsoever—as to what I was going to do, it was decreed by fate that from that time on I was to become an employer.

FAILURE AS MANUFACTURER

## *Don't Live with a Mistake Too Long*

I never dreamed of being in business for myself. In the many years of my experience as a salesman, I felt I was not cut out to be a businessman. I had myself pegged as a salesman, and figured there were special qualifications required to be a businessman. I would have stayed with Maidwell forever if they had not closed down the New York office. I would have stayed with Mr. Poland if I felt I was doing well. In August 1934 I was looking for a job.

The more I thought about matters, the greater my inferiority complex became. I attributed my highly prosperous years with Maidwell from 1929 through 1933 to pure luck. I slipped when I accepted the Perfection connection, and now I felt myself slipping further. I could see myself taking a five thousand dollar a year job for the sake of security. The matter of pride then entered my thoughts. How could I hold my head up and face those who only a few months ago considered me one of the most successful salesmen in the garment industry? Could I tell them that it was a freak, that in reality I never belonged at the top?

Thinking along these lines I finally mustered up enough courage to decide to go into business for myself. I was encouraged by a meeting with Harry Goldman, then buyer and later an executive vice-president of Neisner Brothers, Rochester, New York. He told me of a garment factory already set up complete in Auburn, New York, which I could lease from his father. The idea of being able to go into business without buying a lot of machinery appealed to me and in September I leased it for one year.

Then I inserted an ad in "*Women's Wear,*" our trade paper, for a pattern maker and cutter, also a factory foreman. The first reply to my ad came from Ben Bindler whom I interviewed in mid-September at my home in Forest Hills. I engaged him for fifty dollars a week.

It was a sad day in our lives when we shut the front door of our Stafford Avenue apartment in Forest Hills. Earlier that week we placed our two children in the Kohut School. The morning of the fourth the moving company loaded our furniture to place it in storage. The previous few days we said our "good-byes" to friends and neighbors.

The following day we were set to open our business under my own name, Samuel J. Goldfarb, manufacturer of cotton frocks. A week before Ben Bindler, accompanied by the production man we hired and Ralph Spencer, my young friend whom I met when he caddied for me at the golf course, were at the factory and made preparations for the October fifth opening. From the first day we were there I realized we had made a mistake because all of us were completely ignorant of the producing end of the business. The best setup for a garment plant has the physical layout all on one floor. Then the fabrics can come in from one end, and on an assembly line basis be put through the various operations, so that they leave in shipments to customers on the other end. A one floor operation also makes supervision much easier. The factory we leased was about sixteen feet wide and about seventy feet deep on three floors with no elevator.

The first few nights in Auburn we spent at a hotel. When, however, we considered the dreary prospects for success, we placed ourselves on a Spartan disciplinary living basis. First, we moved to a furnished room for only four dollars a week. Then we figured a budget for our meals which limited the cost of breakfast to twenty cents each, at the cafeteria, and a nominal amount for lunch to permit the luxury of a one dollar and twenty-five cent dinner.

I could write volumes concerning the day to day hardships we encountered in conducting our business. Only a few days after we started to operate we had to dismiss our production man because of complaints from the girls that he was intent on being a Casanova and tried to "wolf" them. It was costing us two and three times as much as our competitors were paying to make similar garments.

The eighty days we stayed in Auburn appeared like years. Even the weather was rugged. The average temperature must have been slightly above zero for the period we were there, with a number of below zero days. We missed the children and often went to bed crying because of our precarious predicament. We were losing money every day. We made dresses we intended to sell for twelve dollars a dozen. Actually they cost us more and were made so poorly that I had to dispose of most of them for four dollars and fifty cents a dozen.

Despite urging from the new friends to stick it out and give it a longer trial, we decided to give up the venture and take our losses. When we came to Auburn we showed an opening net worth of seventeen thousand dollars, almost all in cash. When we left Auburn about December twentieth our worth had dwindled to about ten thousand dollars with practically no cash. It consisted of some cutting machinery, office fixtures and supplies, but chiefly cotton fabrics and trimmings. We rented a loft on Broadway, made arrangements with Clarence Hoover to sew our garments on a flat contract basis of one dollar and seventy-five cents per dozen and readied ourselves to start afresh in New York City.

Having learned the lesson in Auburn that we were ignorant of garment production, we resolved to take care of only that phase of the business which we understood thoroughly and let others who were more expert do the work for which we were unfit. We gave ourselves a new lease on our commercial life by not living with a mistake too long.

BACK TO BROADWAY

## *We Turn the Corner*

On January 2nd, 1935 we opened our Broadway factory where we received all our materials and trimmings, did all the garment cutting and shipped them to contractor Clarence Hoover in New Jersey. When he sewed the cut fabrics into finished garments they were returned to us, where we in turn shipped them to our customers. At 733 Broadway we did our designing and bookkeeping. At 1350 Broadway we paid fifty dollars a month to a Baltimore sportswear firm, for sharing their office where I could spend most of my time selling.

Matters looked grim on the New Year after the disheartening results of my initiation as a manufacturer. When we opened for business on January second I bought a diary to note my appointments and planned activities. On the first page, before attending to my first business transaction, I made this entry—"Vanity, Vanity, All is Vanity," said the preacher in Ecclesiastes. "Only doing service to our fellow men is meaningful."

My reason for making that entry was to remind me

that my striving in business was not to be for shallow reasons of acquiring wealth, power or prestige. Committed to Hillel's doctrine of "Taking care of oneself first, but having done so, to work to better the lot of others," I now proceeded to make a success despite the miserable start I had made.

We made our home in a tiny room at the Herald Square Hotel on Thirty-fourth Street, opposite Macy's. The rate was around fifteen dollars a week. We continued to live on a Spartan scale, allowing ourselves no luxuries. I called Ben Bindler into my office and asked him to accept a ten dollar weekly salary reduction, assuring him that if we regained our losses I would gladly repay him the five hundred and twenty dollars at the end of the year. Ben cheerfully accepted. From the start I felt better under our new set up. The problem of sewing the garments was off our minds. It left room for us to handle the other phases of the business with ease and intelligence. Ben engaged a sweet Italian girl, Lucy Constanza, to be a sample maker. One young man was hired to assist Ben in cutting and another to receive goods and do the shipping. In all there were six of us including Ralph Spencer and me. Ralph did whatever was called for in the cutting and shipping department. Our overhead was nominal. We knew the exact cost of our labor, whereas in Auburn we were ignorant and could never figure costs accurately. We decided to make dresses to wholesale for seven dollars and seventy-five cents a dozen, to retail for one dollar.

We were all young, I being the oldest . . . only thirty-two years of age. Ben Bindler was slightly younger than I, but the others were in their early twenties. All of us worked hard and conscientiously. Having no designer, I did most of the styling.

The highlight of our improved position came in March when I sold all four of our styles to R. H. Macy who displayed them in a Thirty-fourth Street window for a week. I must have gone to look at that window several times each day. It thrilled me to know that only ninety days earlier we were on the brink of failure and now our product was on display at the world's largest store.

With God's aid in 1935 we made up the seven thousand dollar Auburn loss and had a surplus of a few thousand dollars. As I promised Bindler at the start of the year, I restored the five hundred and twenty dollar cut he took and on top of that I gave him a five hundred dollar bonus. We were all elated because we not only retrieved our loss, but gained confidence in ourselves, as a maker of high style cotton dresses to sell for one dollar. We had a feeling that in 1936 we would do even better.

GROWING INTELLECTUAL PAINS

## *Respecting Those Who Know More*

The strain of launching the business anew left me with less time than I desired for reading and study. I was, therefore, grateful for any opportunity afforded me to meet and be with people who were better informed. I remember distinctly one such occasion because of a great lesson my friend Ralph Spencer and I derived from it.

Frank Shames invited Ralph Spencer, Frances and me to visit them on a Sunday afternoon. When we entered their small apartment we found quite a crowd. There were about a dozen men and women including the three of us. I was the oldest as my host, Frank, was about twenty-five years old. The men and women fell into two separate groupings. I sensed that I was in the presence of younger, but far better informed men than I. They were discussing world events with an ease and aplomb I couldn't possibly match. Though a loquacious person, I said little for fear of making a fool of myself. Nat Epstein, a classmate of Frank's, now a top executive of Lerner Shops, and Arnold Beichman, then about twenty, and later to become City Editor of one of New York's liberal publications, dominated the conversation. Beichman was by far the best informed of the group.

It was a most thrilling afternoon for me, and in leaving I expressed my pleasure at meeting the young man who contributed to its success. When we returned to our car Ralph seemed upset. He turned to me and asked how could I possibly have told Arnold Beichman that I was so pleased to meet him and really mean it.

I gave this explanation to Ralph. When I was listening to the discussion and was first exposed to Arnold Beichman's dogmatic, know-it-all manner of speaking, I, too, felt a vehement dislike for the young man. Before permitting this dislike to crystallize I began to question myself, "Why don't you like this young fellow? His appearance? Color of his eyes? Short stature? Tone of voice? Exactly what is it that causes you, an intelligent person, to dislike a human being with whom you have just become acquainted?" Finally the answer came to me. I disliked him because he was superior to me in knowledge and in ability to express himself. "What a terrible reason for disliking anyone, just because he knows more than you do," I censured myself. "That's the type of person you should like, a person who can transmit knowledge and learning to you," I mused to myself. At any rate, after thinking this way a few minutes I took an entirely different attitude toward Arnold. Whereas, previously, his voice irritated me and his words fell on deaf ears, I now found his voice appealing and his words inspiring. By disliking him I would have left that discussion empty minded; by liking him I came away a better informed person. I showed Ralph Spencer that he and I started out the same way—disliking Arnold, but that we wound up altogether differently. He remained with his dislike, while I eradicated the negative feeling to my profit.

Try it yourself the next time you have a negative feeling toward a person. Ask yourself why. In most cases you will, if you are fair minded and objective, conclude that if X has this fault, you have that fault. If X does that disagreeable thing, you can forgive and understand when you consider the circumstances surrounding X. When you overlook the particular error but consider the overall picture of X, you are likely to realize you were mistaken in your negative feeling toward him. Then your attitude will become warm and satisfying for one of the true tests of maturity is the measure of patience and understanding we have in considering others. It brings to mind the statement of the Jewish sage, "Judge every person favorably."

DAVID VERSUS GOLIATH

## *I Create a Slingshot*

It is 1935 and you are making cotton dresses to retail for one dollar. You have only ninety-eight hundred dollars capital and are bucking competitors with hundreds of thousands and, in some cases, several million dollars. How do you do it?

Simple! You remember the story of the delicate David in combat with the monstrous giant, Goliath. You remember David used his noodle and conceived of a slingshot with which he slew Goliath. In business you examine your wares and capitalize not on what you wish you had, but only that which, in fact, you have.

I examined my wares. I had only two cute dresses made for sizes twelve to twenty. I put them in a box under my arm and set out to call on the trade. My first stop was J. J. Newberry Company where I entered the office of a Mr. Homer.

I told Mr. Homer that I had shopped one of his stores the previous Saturday. I was agreeably surprised to find that his stock of cotton dresses to retail for one dollar was, in my opinion, as fine as it was possible to obtain. I wound up saying, "You might well ask what am I seeing you for under the circumstances?" Then I explained that his stock was what I termed bread and butter . . . the desirable fabrics and styles wanted by the vast majority of customers, but that I had a little paprika to add a little spice.

I was asked to show him the paprika and pulled out the two cute styles which I dangled in front of him.

He said, "Young man, you surely have a fresh angle. Most salesmen tell me I should replace part of my selection with their superior line, but you tell me everything I have is good."

In any case, Mr. Homer gave me a trial order for one hundred of his top stores and, happily, the dresses proved spicy and resulted in my enjoying a close relationship with Newberry stores for many years thereafter.

GOING INTO BUSINESS FUND

## *Unique Advice to An Employee*

My production man, Ben Bindler, too, sensed the fact that we were on the road to success in the dollar dress business. One day he asked me about the advisability of buying a little house. I told him not to do so. I told him that in the garment business it was natural for an employee to aspire to go into business for himself some day. There were, I told him, a number of reasons for it. First, because most people engaged in the business are Jews. They are strong individualists by nature, and can't stand regimentation, or a feeling of being subservient to anyone. I explained that this was a good trait and a mark of a more highly civilized person. Analyzing the peoples of the world, one finds that the more backward and ignorant are more regimented, while the people with a tradition of freedom and learning are more individualistic. That is why the American is more of an individualist than the European, and the European more so than the Asiatic or African. Another reason why employees in the needle industry hunger to go into business for themselves is that one can start with small capital. Thus an employee can estimate how little it took to start the business. Finally, there is the matter of intimacy between employer and employee.

Take as an example my own business. There were only a handful of us operating it, all in very close contact with one another. Every employee knew how much goods was bought, how many garments made, how many sold, to whom they were sold, and it didn't take much arithmetic to figure how much the boss was making. So I told Ben he would be foolish to buy a house. I urged that he resolve to save his money and that he should ear-mark the first ten thousand dollars he accumulated as a "Going into Business Fund." After that I told him he could buy a house, or do anything else he desired with his money.

The wise employer should take it for granted that key employees hope some day to enter business for themselves. He should treat them so well, compensate them generously and make them so happy that they will want to stay with him forever.

MR. G., CAN I HAVE A RAISE?

## *She Almost Sold Her Birthright for a Mess of Pottage*

In the mid-thirties, as we were emerging from the worst depression we had ever experienced, my secretary, Freda Raab, was being paid forty dollars a week. Considering that only two years earlier Freda started at fourteen dollars weekly, she was making excellent progress.

Nevertheless, returning from lunch one day she asked to speak to me in my office. She seemed to be perturbed as she blurted out, "Mr. Goldfarb, don't you think I ought to have a raise?" I said, "Freda, I haven't thought about it. If I had felt you were entitled to one I should have given it to you."

Freda went on to say that she had lunch with three other girls all of whom were secretaries in the same building. One of the four, a Miss Martha, left the group earlier and the other three started to talk about her. It developed that she was earning fifty dollars weekly working for the YZ Company. The two girls told Freda that she was every bit as capable as Martha. Now Freda pointed out to me that she thought she too should be earning fifty dollars a week.

I listened carefully while I observed the young lady's nervousness. It was apparent to me that Freda's heart was not in this request. I made this startling proposition to her. I said, "You ask for a ten dollar raise so you can match Martha's fifty dollars. I'll go you one better. I'll give you sixty dollars a week and will always pay you ten dollars more per week than Martha earns."

Freda's eyes brightened. She was all smiles. She expressed her gratitude and remarked, "Really, Mr. Goldfarb, I didn't expect anything as wonderful as this. I would have been satisfied with fifty dollars." Thus she left my office beaming and happy.

The following day Freda Raab contacted me early in the morning. I noted no gaiety or cheer. She seemed crestfallen and sad as she said, "Mr. Goldfarb, I plead with you to forget the agreement we made yesterday. I insist on staying on the forty dollar scale and will never again ask you for a raise."

When I asked for an explanation she told me that when she reported it to her husband and mother the previous night they said there must be a catch to the deal. They began considering what the catch might be and Freda herself figured it out. Knowing me so intimately because she typed all my letters she knew it was burdensome to periodically evaluate the compensation of my employees. This plan relating to her and Martha made it very simple for me. Freda was smart enough to conclude that in the long run she would be getting the worst of the deal. In other words, it might be as in the case of Esau in the Bible who "sold his birthright for a mess of pottage."

In any case, she persuaded me to forget the entire matter. This proved to be a brilliant decision. Some years later when Martha was earning only eighty-five dollars on her secretarial job, Freda Raab, as vice-president and piece goods buyer for our company, was earning fifteen thousand dollars a year.

### I NEED PAISLEY BUT BUY SCROLL PRINT

## *I Resolve to Pay for My Mistakes*

Early in 1936 our business boomed. We more than doubled our shipments of the first three months in 1935. Naturally, as business booms, one is disposed to be less cautious in expenditures and buying. I recall one incident clearly to prove this point. I went down to Worth Street, the textile fabric market, with the specific purpose of buying a paisley pattern which was in great demand at that time. I walked into Borden's on the corner of Broadway and Worth Street and could not find a paisley. I walked across the street into Jacob Bernheimer's. There my close friend, Bill Milius, succeeded in selling me fifty thousand yards of a scroll pattern.

I walked out of the store with the copy of the order in my pocket. I had not taken ten steps when I realized I had made the wrong purchase. I hadn't taken fifty steps when it occurred to me that I was, for all intents and purposes, stuck with fifty thousand yards of an unwanted, no-place-in-mind-for-it pattern. I turned around with the idea of going back and asking Bill Milius to destroy the order, as it was not even close to what I wanted. Instead, I stopped short and began to ask questions of myself. I decided that there was nothing unethical in asking Bill to cancel an order which wasn't five minutes old. I would be doing no injury to him or his company, for they had not yet taken any action with reference to it. In fact, I knew that when I explained to Bill that by yielding to his pressure selling I would do harm to myself, he would insist on cancelling it. Nevertheless, I decided to remain stuck with the fifty thousand yards. It wasn't false pride that kept me from cancelling.

The reason I decided to remain stuck with a purchase even if it meant a loss was that I did not want to go through life having other people pay for my mistakes. How would I ever learn to avoid making mistakes if I could easily and without penalty get out of them? I said to myself, "Sam Goldfarb, it may be a costly lesson, but if it will teach you to avoid making that or a similar mistake again it will be well worth the price you will pay." It took the better part of a prosperous year such as 1936 to merchandise and get rid of the fifty thousand yards of the scroll pattern. It cost me time and money to learn that whenever we make a purchase for our business we must have a definite plan in mind for the use of it. Over the years it has paid me big dividends to adhere to my determination that no one shall ever be permitted to pay for my mistakes.

THE GIRL WAS NAIVE

## *The Answer Was Forthright*

One day in talking to our sample maker, she said to me, "Mr. Goldfarb, it must make you happy to realize that you make it possible for women to get such exceptional style and value for only a dollar." I turned to Lucy and answered, "My dear girl, I wish I could truthfully say yes to your comment. You happen to be wrong. It would make me happy if, when I designed and planned to produce those dresses, I did so primarily because I wanted to serve the consumer. That, however, is not the case."

"Why do I make these pretty dresses . . . these wonderful values? I do so because I want to fill my pockets with gold. The fact that the consumer is happy to get my product is incidental." Then I went on to philosophize on the subject Lucy had brought to mind. I told her that there was a principle involved in the topic we were discussing which was responsible for all the happenings in our civilization. It was because everyone in business, like myself, was seeking to fill his pockets with money, that we have as a consequence, depressions and wars. "Ah," I went on to say, "when the time comes that the producer gives only minor thought to profit and primary consideration to serving the consumer we shall have a civilization that will be conducive to peace and good will."

## I WANT TO ABANDON BUSINESS FOR LABOR

## *David Dubinsky Counsels Me Wisely*

The year 1936 wound up amazingly profitable. It was our second full year in business and our volume of two hundred and twelve thousand dollars in 1935 was far more than doubled. Like a cub lion tasting blood for the first time, I felt my success whetting my desire to roll up my sleeves and really start doing big business during 1937. I had ideas galore and, in fact, 1937 proved to be a most eventful year in many ways. But as the saying goes, "Man proposes and God disposes." It happened that many of my plans were frustrated.

Early in the year when I considered the implication of my plans to forge ahead and expand my business, I became conscience stricken and concluded it was parasitical for me to think in terms of more material advancement. Events abroad were tragic. Hitler was showing his vile hand. In our country one heard and read much about "labor racketeering." This impressed me very much. I had always felt that the future of America rested on a labor movement which was big and powerful but at the same time honorable and discreet. I felt that the gains which labor had made in the previous thirty years were threatened by its unsavory element, the racketeers. I had an overwhelming urge to do something to help annihilate everything sinister in the labor movement, which since the advent of President Roosevelt's New Deal had made such impressive gains. The Congress of Industrial Organization had come into being only a few years before and was already rivaling the old established American Federation of Labor.

A conflict was raging within me. On the one hand, I wanted to go ahead in business and do big things; on the other hand, I could mark time in my business . . . leave it to my associates to operate on a small scale, while I joined the C.I.O. as an organizer for the purpose of helping it to rid itself of the racketeering element. I decided to serve the people rather than myself and arranged for a meeting with David Dubinsky at his office. I told Dubinsky of my belief that a successful young business man consecrated to the task of helping to fight the saboteuring elements in labor's own ranks could render a real service. I had taken it for granted that I would be welcomed with out-stretched arms. To my amazement Dubinsky discouraged me and thought the idea unrealistic. He told me my case reminded him of the rich and beautiful Mexican heiress who had come to see him in San Antonio, Texas, where an organizing campaign was being conducted with the Garment Workers, most of whom were Mexicans. She, too, wanted to be an organizer. Dubinsky told her to look at herself in the mirror—to look at her soft hands and well-manicured fingernails. Dubinsky told her the workers would consider it ludicrous to listen to someone bent on organizing them if that person failed to exhibit evidence of being hardy and tough. They would pay little heed to someone like the Mexican heiress who was beautiful, soft and obviously far removed from the workers' arena of living.

For the same reason Dubinsky felt that I would be looked upon with skepticism and cynicism by the workers if I attempted to talk to them about organizing. Though he admired the ideal motive for my visit with him, he felt certain it was not realistic and he suggested I stick to the business of making money. He added, "The liberals could use a few solvent supporters."

A CRISIS IN THE FAMILY

## *We Seize the Opportunity*

Our third son, Alan, was born on the twenty-third of December, 1937. From the day of his birth he gave us much anxiety. He could not swallow the milk fed to him by breast or bottle. After each feeding he would vomit all his food.

He had what the surgeon who subsequently operated on him called a pyloric stenosis. In a normal child the tube leading to the stomach has the circumference of a lead pencil. In Alan's case the tube was as small as the lead in a pencil.

Not being able to retain food he gained no weight in ten weeks and it was necessary to operate on him. Dr. George Schwartz, who had operated on President Eisenhower opened Alan's stomach and performed a successful operation.

Thank God, he survived, but made little progress in the five years thereafter. He still regurgitated and was given twenty instead of eight bottles daily in order to retain some food. He was on the bottle for five years.

When Alan was six his weight was that of a three-year-old child. His body was proportioned like one less than half his age. We took him to a member of the faculty of Harvard Medical College. This eminent pediatrician said that Alan would be a midget and never reach three feet in height.

Learning of this my family was stunned. That evening my middle son, Murray, said to me, "Dad, you taught us that crisis spells opportunity. Tell me where is it in this terrible crisis?"

My answer was that we cannot wage war with God. We must resign ourselves to His will. Confronted, however, with a handicapped child we have the opportunity to become kinder, more loving, more patient and above all, more understanding.

As a matter of fact, I believe my sons have developed into better human beings because of their exposure for many years to a tiny brother who looked to them for help.

Fortunately it was God's will that Alan grow out of his handicapped start. It was painfully slow and he was always far below normal in size until his fifteenth year. Thereafter he shot up so that when he was eighteen he attained the normal height of five feet six.

Today, thank God, he is happily married and doing a spendid job in the family business.

RESPECTING MY BROTHER'S WISHES

## *Proving That Two Heads Are Better Than One*

During my negotiations with the International Ladies' Garment Workers Union I acted on the advice of my brother, Abe, which probably altered the entire course of my business career.

I reported to him daily about the conferences between the Union leaders and the New York City Housedress Manufacturers. Finally the day of decision arrived. The manufacturers were going to take action and it appeared as if they would sign on the Union's terms.

As I was leaving my office to go to Union headquarters, my brother called back and said, "Kid, would you do your older brother a favor? Promise me that before taking a pen in your hand to sign on the dotted line, you will put it down and excuse yourself. Then you will go to the nearest telephone and call me."

I kept my promise. As my competitors were standing in line waiting to sign the Union contract, I went downstairs to the nearest telephone booth and called Abe. My brother then said. "Look here, Son, they won't put you in jail if you wait another twenty-four hours to think this matter over. You have taken my advice so far, now complete the job by coming right back to the office to talk things over."

On my return to the office we tried to figure how to get an out of town factory set up that would take care of our needs. I telephoned Mr. Poland of Perfection Garment Company, Martinsburg, West Virginia. I told him of my difficulties and asked him what chance there was for working out some suitable deal. He was thrilled. He shot back a quick answer to the effect that I could name my own terms; that he would be delighted to make my product. In a matter of days my entire equipment was moved from New York to Martinsburg, West Virginia. Now I no longer required the services of contractors, as my garments were cut, made and shipped under Mr. Poland's supervision.

By respecting my brother's wishes I became more successful than had I not listened to him, proving that generally two heads are better than one.

## THE MOST TRAGIC PICTURE I EVER SAW

### *I Am Converted to the Doctrine of Love*

The strain I underwent in watchful waiting and praying for my baby Alan before and after his operation was only the beginning of a year that was to test my faith and morale.

During 1938 I went into an aggressive opening of twenty-one cotton dress shops. I lost every dollar I invested.

It proved to be the most trying year of my life. In retrospect I can say that I went through a transformation truly unique and frightening. It was, however, a most wonderful experience.

The "straw that broke the camel's back" was a picture I saw in a newspaper. It showed Jewish men in Vienna wearing frock coats and silk hats, down on their knees scrubbing the streets while their Nazi tormentors were standing by laughing in hyena-like fashion. Like Moses who rose to righteous wrath and indignation when he saw his Jewish brethren beaten in Egypt, like Lincoln who did something about it when he saw the sale of Negro slaves on the auction block, so I resolved never to be at peace with myself until I did everything possible to fight the evil which brought about such sadistic and savage acts.

For months I carried this picture in my wallet. I would take it out before mealtime and look at it while asking myself, "What are you going to do about this?" Only when I assured my conscience that I would do my very best to fight this wicked Nazism could I allow myself to partake of food. To fight the evils of Nazism I did some philosophizing. What sort of human beings were these Jews on their knees? Were those who persecuted them men or monkeys? What was happening to a world that permitted such outrages? Was there a single American who would fail to express his indignation at seeing such a picture? The sad truth was that millions of Americans were so morally bankrupt that they enjoyed seeing that picture. Why? Why had nineteen hundred years of Christianity proven such a failure? In my search for the truth I wanted to be objective. I gave critical evaluation to the persecuted as well as to the persecutors.

Why were Jews persecuted? After countless hours of thinking about it I arrived at this conclusion. Jews were persecuted because they failed to hold sacred a covenant they made with God at Mount Sinai. Tradition tells us that God had offered the "Torah" to other nations, all of whom refused it. The Jews accepted it and promised that they would revere it and adhere to it. They did not fulfill this promise. Instead of leading exemplary lives that would serve as a model for others the Jews lived just as everyone else—no better, no worse. Persecution of Jews would cease only when they kept the promise given to God. How would it come to pass that Jews as a nation would lead the type of life that would inspire other nations to a higher standard? Only when they had a land of their own. In such a nation the political, economic and spiritual conditions would be conducive to self-fulfillment. This would enable the Jews to make good their promise. Jews all over the world would be respected because of their extraordinary achievements. I was convinced that Jews must work toward the establishment of a homeland in Palestine.

Having resolved the Jewish problem I now considered other evils in the world. Power! Power! Overseas Stalin, Hitler, Mussolini and others seized it to benefit themselves. In America labor leaders, newspaper publishers and heads of giant corporations sought power for themselves. President Roosevelt was fighting to preserve power in America for the people, poor and rich, black and white, and Jew and Gentile.

I concluded that what was needed was the moral regeneration of mankind. People must return to practice the ethical values basic in all religious teaching. It would be a good world if men took seriously the admonition to love their neighbor, to do unto others as they would have others do unto them! The prophets of the Old Testament, Jesus, Mohammed, Buddha and leaders of all religions preached the Golden Rule as the way that leads to brotherhood and peace. Since we were living in a highly commercial age I thought it might be well to coin a slogan that would put the Golden Rule into words better suited for the market place. I wondered why on Sunday people attending church services reached a high state of idealism, but conducted themselves differently throughout the week. This gave birth to my slogan, "Do Business on Monday in the Spirit of Sunday." I had great hopes of popularizing it.

Business was secondary in my thoughts. Day and night I was thinking about the atrocious conditions abroad, as Hitler became more ruthless. I felt that if he were not stopped it would lead to a Second World War that would be more devastating than World War I. It made me sick at heart to observe Americans going about their business paying no heed to the menace that threatened civilization. Hitler and hate became an obsession with me.

I had the feeling of being inspired by God to exterminate hate from my being. I concluded that I should never again hate a single human being—not even Hitler.

The prophet's admonition would be taken literally by me, "Hate sin but not the sinner—hate evil but not the evil-doer."

I hated and despised Hitler's cruelty; I abhorred Nazism, fascism, communism; but I would not hate Nazis, fascists or communists. One pitied and understood those who did evil but one should not hate them. For to hate a single human being could enable one to hate many.

Now I understood the action taken by a mathematics instructor at the University of Pennsylvania. The headlines read: "Slain child's dad asks help for killer." The news item continued: "The grieving father of a slain three-year-old daughter today offered understanding and help to the fifteen-year-old honor student who confessed the killing. The father said, 'Yesterday afternoon I lost the most precious thing that life ever gave me—a three-and-a-half-year-old girl child. She was murdered. Had I caught the boy in the act, I would have wished to kill him. Now that there is no undoing of what is done, I only wish to help him. Let no feeling of caveman vengeance influence us.'"

Twenty-six years have passed since I made the resolution to hate evil but not the evil-doer. I have had countless experiences of being double-crossed and dealt with shabbily. It never occurs to me to hate the doer. I have only sympathy and understanding for such depraved minds.

Two high-placed men left my employ and apparently had no other idea for succeeding except to copy my models, price them for less and go to my customers to undersell and destroy me. Nevertheless, I prospered and they went broke. I did not glory in their downfall. I had them return to work for me without ever saying a negative word to them.

This book being a heritage to my children, I appeal to them, to my grandchildren and all who come thereafter never to hate another human being. They may not appreciate or like the person. They need not embrace or show affection for the wrong-doer. They should, however, understand and sympathize with all those who sin.

God help them to be guided by the age-old concept, "Hate evil but not the evil-doer."

## DOWN FOR THE COUNT OF NINE

### *J. C. Penney Saves My Business*

Returning from a trip in May I found things were going from bad to worse. We were already committed to fabrics which were not wanted and were forced to operate with them through the summer season. When the June figures were handed to me by my accountants they made sad reading. We had lost more than half our investment. To add to my difficulties my stylist and production man left to go into business for themselves. The crisis in my financial position was reached at the end of July. After liquidating the summer dresses, I was left with no cash and an ill assorted stock of piece goods. The situation looked quite hopeless. The lightning success and profits I made from 1935 through 1937 were almost entirely dissipated during 1938.

This is the way matters stood at the end of July 1938. My business showed a net worth of only thirty-five thousand dollars but was tied up in merchandise difficult to sell. Business was at a standstill. My stylist and production man were now competing against me. The situation was made even gloomier by the fact that the naturally poor fall season was staring me in the face. I had no cash, no ideas, no selling organization, no spirit to continue the business. Had anyone come along in July 1938 and offered me twenty-five thousand cash for my entire worldly possessions I would have eagerly accepted and gone to California to get away from the scene of my adversity. Twenty years later I would not have accepted five million dollars for my enterprises.

Most everyone in and outside of the industry was pitying or ridiculing me because they pointed to my failure as proof that idealism has no place in business. I knew that it was not because of my idealism but the fact that carrying it to the extreme had resulted in the failure of my business. I concluded that if I survived the precarious predicament I was in I would practice my ideals but moderate the preachment of my philosophy so that it did not interfere with business.

Then lady luck smiled out loud on me and raised me from disillusionment and despair to a liquid position and hope. I developed a short group of high styled cotton dresses for misses. I went to the J. C. Penney Company who operate sixteen hundred stores and told them I would confine to them the label used in those styles which I had registered under the name Four Star Hollywood Pre Vue Frocks. The label was a natural for garments that were highly styled. I had done no business with the Penney company. Now when I couldn't get business from my regular accounts they gave me a twenty thousand dollar order. That order came at a time when everything seemed hopeless and meant more to me than the three hundred and forty-five thousand dollar order on Hollywood Pre Vue Frocks placed by the Penney Company in July 1948. In the years that have passed since that first order we have done many millions of dollars worth of business with the J. C. Penney Company to our mutual profit. I shall always be grateful to them for saving the life of my business.

DOROTHY THOMPSON

## *She Paid Me the Greatest Compliment*

In 1941 I entered into another stage of activities to broaden my interests. This was attending testimonial dinners for great personalities, which, of course, meant contributing to the institutions sponsoring the affairs. It was gratifying to participate in sponsoring the Bernard Baruch dinner and Freedom House honoring Wendell Willkie.

The greatest testimonial I ever attended was the one given to Dorothy Thompson in 1941, at the height of her brilliant career as a great liberal.

On the dais were seated Mrs. Sara Delano Roosevelt, Governor Herbert Lehman, Wendell Willkie and representatives from practically every country on the globe. Letters from Mahatma Gandhi and Winston Churchill were read. She was referred to as "first lady of the universe."

Imagine my pleasure when Meyer Weisgal, with the Weizmann Institute in Israel, invited me to lunch with Dorothy Thompson. Thereafter I had some interesting meetings with her at her home.

Once when we were alone I said, "Dorothy, I can't understand why one who has access to the world's greatest people finds it necessary to contact a simple dress manufacturer when you seek financial aid for one of your causes." I continued, "People will say you are a stooge for the Jews since you are mostly in their company." Dorothy turned to me, "See that chair you are sitting on? Only yesterday the senior head of a foremost banking firm was sitting on it! When I broached the subject of the cause his reaction was as cold as the granite which comes from the state where he was born. When I want immediate action instead of evasive promises, I know I can get it from your people rather than from the multimillionaire bankers." When the records were considered I had to acknowledge that she was probably right.

The greatest compliment of my life was paid to me by Dorothy Thompson. On leaving her house she took me to the door and we parted after she said to me, "Sam, I have traveled the better part of the world as author and correspondent, I have met fanatical Communists as well as fanatical Fascists. You, however, are the first fanatical democrat I have ever met."

During Roosevelt's 1944 campaign for the presidency, Dorothy, commenting over the radio, criticized F.D.R.'s famous Teamsters Union speech in which he mentioned Fala, his pet dog. I wrote to her and explained why I thought she was unfair. Without delay Miss Thompson replied and admitted the validity of my criticism. Moreover, she asked that I listen the following Saturday night to an important speech she was to make and which would rectify the wrong done in her previous talk. Most of the experts who were working in Roosevelt's behalf, told me they rated Dorothy's Saturday night speech as the best of the entire campaign.

Currently the book by Vincent Sheehan telling of her marriage to Sinclair Lewis is worth reading.

## MY SON IS PUNISHED FOR LYING

### *Don't Call Me Sam*

Having moved from Forest Hills to 115 Central Park West, New York in 1943, we entered our two oldest boys in Columbia Grammar School in Manhattan.

At school my boys were just fair students. Their relationship with me, however, was not ordinary. Gene and Murray would often tell me that many of their friends envied them because of the ideal father-son life we enjoyed.

My sons knew the story of my youth. I felt, and time proved me to be correct, that it would help them develop into men without going through the tortuous guilt feelings I had experienced as a child. One of my great aims in life was to give my sons the rare luxury of going through the stages of adolescence and youth without any complexes.

It was, therefore, a shock and surprise when I discovered my son Murray telling me a lie. I could only attribute it to the fact that he had acquired several friends who did not wield a good influence on him.

One night Frances and I returned to our apartment at about eleven thirty P.M. and found Murray with five other boys playing cards in our breakfast room. Murray was about seventeen years old. I commented on the late hour and in defense Murray ignored the time, but simply referred to the fact that they were playing black jack for only a cent a point. I told them it was wrong for them to play cards any night during the week when the time could be better used for study. The game broke up and I called Murray into Gene's room where the latter was "burning the midnight oil" in preparation for an exam. I then gave them a lecture on the subject of gambling which I felt left its mark on them.

Retiring to my bedroom, I told Frances I had a feeling I had perhaps been a little severe with the boys who so seldom gave us cause for concern. I decided to tiptoe back to Murray's room to reassure him in order to put his mind completely at ease. Passing through Alan's bedroom and entering the bathroom adjoining the older boys' room I overheard Murray saying to Gene, "Dad's right. It is wrong to use a night of the school week for card playing. I wonder what he would have said if he knew we were playing for a nickel a point." I was stunned. I turned on the bathroom light and expressed my sadness at learning that he had lied to me. I told him I was unprepared to tell him what form his punishment would take, but he could be assured it would be severe.

In the morning I was inspired with an idea for punishing Murray. I said to him, "I am not cutting your allowance or depriving you of anything material. From now on I forbid you to call me 'Sam.' I now insist that you address me formally as 'Dad' or 'Father.' "

For the following two days I could see that Murray was going through a tortuous mental state. On the third night after his card game, Murray asked to see me alone in the library. Bursting into tears he said he could not endure the punishment. He could not understand its significance when I first spoke to him about it, but with the passing of every hour he felt the strain was unbearable. He could not endure a relationship with me that was less than perfect. He must have the privilege of calling me "Sam." He promised he would never lie to me, but with a twinkle in his eyes said, "But remember, Sam, you don't have to question me about everything."

## RELIGIOUS INSTRUCTION IN PUBLIC SCHOOLS? NO!

### *Teach Character Development There? Yes!*

In the mid-thirties Dr. Robinson, President of the City College of New York, was the guest speaker at one of the regular forum meetings of the Forest Hills Jewish Center. His subject was Child Delinquency. I raised the point that if character education was taught in our public schools it would lessen the development of delinquency. Dr. Robinson's answer was that character development should be left to the church, and more particularly, to the parents.

I said that it was dangerous to rely on the Joneses with large families to instruct their children and that church dogma and ritual would fail to do the job effectively.

In the thirty years that have passed I am more firmly convinced than ever that one of the most important areas for character building should be the public schools.

Let me make it clear that I do not approve of religion being taught in our public schools. I fully agree with our Supreme Court ruling that in a democracy it is unconstitutional to teach that which might be inimical to any sect, even Atheists.

Why should prayers, dogmas or rituals of any dominant group be taught the children of a democratic society? Why not teach universal ethics that will appeal to and benefit all children?

I visualize character education in the public schools starting in kindergarten. Games would be set up in a manner to give the teacher an opening to point out the difference between good and bad sportsmanship, fair play and sharing.

As the child entered different grades the instruction

would be given commensurate with the child's ability to understand and learn. In the second grade a child could be taught that we love our neighbor and that no distinction be made of tall or short, white or black, Jew or Gentile, but that all human beings are our neighbors. The fact that it was the admonition of Leviticus, Jesus or Confucius need not be mentioned. What's the difference if it is Mrs. Cunningham, their teacher, who says it?

Above all the child should be taught that to hate another human being is a throwback to animalism. A decent human being must hate evil, but not the evil doer.

Confucianism, Buddhism, Judaism and Christianity have been taught for thousands of years. To what extent has this teaching taught its adherents love of neighbor and the despicability of hate? Hate is more rampant today than ever in the history of man. President Kennedy's assassination drew the attention of all mankind to this truth.

Is there any doubt that if character training had been part of public education for the past hundred years there would be far less hate and prejudice in our midst?

Isn't a society rotten and insane to permit instructors or teachers to teach hatred of individuals or groups? In Germany, for decades before Hitler, it was common to find college professors teaching their students that Jews ought to be hated. Some professors at the world renowned Heidelberg openly taught hatred of Jews with the result that three students on June 24, 1922 murdered Reich minister of Foreign Affairs, Walter Rathenau, because he was a Jew.

Two of the assassins committed suicide. The third served time in jail, then joined the French Foreign Legion. He became adjutant-chief and one day, addressing four Jewish legionnaires, said, "I know you fellows think I dislike you as most non-coms around here do. But that isn't true. I love all Jews. In my opinion they belong to the finest and most gifted people in the world." The full story about this adjutant-chief appeared in *Harper's* magazine in April 1943. In my opinion it is the most remarkable true story that has ever been told. I have distributed thousands of copies and hope some day to have a play about it produced on Broadway.

It is the story of how a man, taught to hate Jews, murders the foremost Jew in his country, then finally learns that his professors were madmen, and says: "The Nazis had falsified all the facts about the Jews in order to get a pretext for continuing excesses."

The Nazis murdered six million innocent Jews and subsequently the Adenauer led Bonn government repents and pays restitution to the State of Israel.

Henry Ford spent a fortune publishing the *Dearborn Independent* teaching hatred of Jews and then apologized in court.

Now, after almost two thousand years, the Catholic Church corrects a vicious crime by removing anything negative to Jews in their teaching. True, it is never too late to correct a mistake, but consider the Inquisition and the tens upon tens of thousands of Jews that were killed and tortured because of this false Catholic doctrine.

What am I driving at? That millions and millions of innocent Jews have been slaughtered because church and state permitted hate to be taught to the young. Kill first and repent later has been the pattern for centuries.

It will never end until leaders in government and of the church have such abhorrence for hate that commencing in kindergarten, all the way through college, children be taught that only loving one's neighbor makes one worthy of being labelled a man.

## BROADWAY OR MAIN STREET

## . . . *Vanity Versus Sanity*

From the day I arrived in New York in 1929 to the present my place of business has been located on Broadway. It's a wonderful street in many ways but in this particular chapter I refer to it as it is believed to be by those who do not live in nor have ever been to New York City. What does Broadway mean to them? Glamor, glitter, crowds, the theater, actors and actresses, the arts, artists and models, movies, gigantic neon signs, dance halls, bars and all else that adds up to excitement, sophistication and fun.

I fear that Americans are becoming increasingly more Broadway minded and I believe this to be a threat to the good and welfare of our country. To me Broadway is razzle-dazzle, hocus-pocus, humpty-dumpty and we're headed for a fall if we fail to understand that too much Broadway mindedness is a curse that will weaken the character of future generations.

Empires fell long before hydrogen bombs were created. Witness Rome, once the greatest. Why did it go to the dogs? Because vanity rather than sanity motivated the behaviour of the people. Throughout history we read of mighty nations collapsing and ending as fourth rate powers. Material elevation too often results in spiritual degradation.

Broadwayites are on a spree. Making money and spending it seems to be all that they have on their minds. God is ignored. The lust for pleasure dominates and the people cast aside the simple, natural means of enjoyment. Everyone appears to be in search of a thrill. Flamboyancy, grotesquerie and hubbub seem to pervade the air.

Where will it lead? Consider what has happened to our music, the dance, our painting and literature that emanate from Broadway. Coarseness and vulgarity reign supreme. With a start such as was given to us decades ago by Sigmund Romberg, Irving Berlin, Jerome Kern, Cole Porter, George Gershwin and others of their ilk, why are we exposed to so much claptrap, moaning, groaning and clamor that pass for today's music? Rodgers and Hammerstein, Lerner and Loewe have shown dedication to simplicity, sweetness and rhythm. For the most part, however, our air waves today are a profusion of noise.

The twist and that which has followed certainly fails to reflect a forward moving society. Rather it suggests a thoughtless, uninspired, care-about-nothing attitude, ready and willing to latch on to anything providing it is vulgar or pornographic. Irene Castle, one of the greatest ballroom dancers America ever saw pronounced the twist "disgraceful, unbecoming and hideous."

Now we come to this thing called "modern art." With rare exception I believe it to be "sick" art emanating from sick minds. Three words come to mind when one coolly endeavors to analyze the significance of those terrible pictures so widely exhibited: abstract, anarchy and existentialism. My dictionary defines abstract as "not easy to understand . . . loosely theoretical and not practical." Anarchy is defined as "disorder in any sphere of activity." The definition of existentialism . . . "it holds that each man exists as an individual in a purposeless universe and that he must oppose his hostile environment through the exercise of his free will."

Do you see what I see? Unkempt beards, untidy rooms, empty beer cans, sloppy clothes, slovenly gait and an overall roguish appearance. Can't you hear foul language, cynically expressed and a I-don't-give-a-damn-for anything or anyone attitude? *Newsweek,* April 13th, 1964, quotes 73-year-old V. W. Van Gogh, nephew of the great Van Gogh and a great artist in his own right as saying, "Professional artists are unhappy men."

Living in Sarasota, Florida in one of the great Art Center's of America let me say in fairness that the artists I meet are not at all like those I described in the paragraph above. I feel certain that not only in small towns of America, but even abroad, artists are not misfits nor much different in appearance and manner from the rest of the population.

Greenwich Village in New York is where many artists live or congregate. I choose for the purpose of my theme to make Broadway the "scapegoat." So too would I consider Soho in London and Place Pigalle in Paris. I do not deny that I seek to paint Broadway, Soho and Place Pigalle as the Sodom and Gomorrah of today's world.

They symbolize for me the negative, wicked and phony developments that have progressed much too far and too fast to suit the decent majority in our society.

I subscribe wholeheartedly to the pronouncement made by a group of Catholic bishops who said, "Powerful factions are trying to revive an 'anything goes' policy in movie production and make nudity and sex perversion standard elements for film treatment."

They object to films that "condone and even promote premarital sexual indulgence." Further says the report, "counterfeit film artists are making increasingly blatant attempts to 'attract an audience by directly stimulating base emotional responses of an erotic or violent nature'."

Finally it says, "Mature and sophisticated people may be able to resist such influences, but for the young the stimulation of one such film frequently becomes an immediate occasion of sin."

To such pronouncements I say, "Hallelujah!" over and over again. I have four young grandchildren. I dread to think of what they may be exposed to in a decade from now when they are in their teens.

Everything these bishops said about films applies to much of the literature sweeping the nation today.

Last night I picked up a book given reviews that I could only hope for my own book . . . by two of the most powerful critics in America. I had hoped to have the stamina and patience to read through to the finish, but abandoned the book after about forty pages. The use of obscene four letter words and references to acts of sex perversion were sickening. I am not straitlaced or prudish, I have sympathy and understanding for those not fortunate to be born with normal, healthy sex desires. I nevertheless rebel at seeing in print language and reference to sex acts which turn my stomach and which I know would be injurious to the immature and unsophisticated reader.

The supreme court justices can devise ways and means of keeping these pornographic books from being read by their grandchildren. What about the masses? Do the judges see no danger in teenage girls in the lower economic brackets reading about a girl like themselves becoming rich and famous via the road of prostitution? The author makes it abundantly clear that from a teenager to a dowager the heroine has had nothing but fun all along the scarlet road.

It seems to me that the simple test for a judge to make in determining what books are to be banned is simply to ask himself, "Might this book do harm to my child? . . . to my grandchild?" It is now an academic matter since the kind of books being published are so pornographic that I can't conceive of anything lower on the scale of morality for judges to be concerned with.

We can only hope that the "flood" will be halted; that the courts keep additional books of the type we've discussed from being published and that we are all fortunate in supervising the reading habits of our children.

I have contended that the advance of Broadwayhood and the decline of Main Street largely accounts for the decay in morality of our songs, dances, arts and literature. I'd be a fool to intimate that Main Street is pure white, and Broadway jet black. I do not presume to paint the small towns of America as being altogether virtuous. Sinclair Lewis and Grace Metallious tried in *Main Street* and *Peyton Place* to show that evil abounds in the small towns as well as the large cities.

It is my firm belief, however, that the degree of looseness and immorality is increasing by geometric progression in the climate of Broadway and is comparatively mild and manageable in the quiet, clear atmosphere of Main Street.

I would like to see it come about that the decent majority make themselves vocal and highly critical of beatniks and odd balls. Treat them as a menace rather than as a joke. Parents should do all in their power to point to the more sensible way of life of the small towners who prefer simplicity of living and old-fashioned simple virtues.

In short our youth must become committed to the truth that America needs less vanity and more sanity. America needs less of the nonsense called Broadway and more of the horse sense called Main Street.

## BECOMING POLITICALLY CONSCIOUS

### *I Pay Seven Thousand Dollars to Speak Seven Minutes*

One morning in the fall of 1944 I received a telephone call from Mr. Samuel Hoffman, the dean of all housedress makers. "Sam," he went on to say, "would you like to join me for lunch at the Lawyers Club where Henry Wallace is making a talk in behalf of F.D.R.?"

I joined Mr. Hoffman and on our way downtown he said, "Sam, I must warn you that there will be a campaign to raise funds after Mr. Wallace's speech." I told him that I had never contributed a dollar to any political campaign and I had no intention of doing so now.

My friend went on to explain that perhaps I did not understand. He said, "You gave ten thousand dollars to one charity that you are interested in this year. No doubt you supported dozens of other causes in moderate amounts. What objection do you have to supporting a candidate for President of the United States in such a critical period in our history?"

I learned that Mr. Hoffman planned to contribute one hundred dollars at the luncheon and it was not tax deductible. Then I told him that since the amount was nominal I would probably go along and make my first political contribution.

The luncheon was sponsored by an organization called the Political Action Committee and was headed by Sidney Hillman, a prominent labor leader. Henry Wallace made a stirring talk that impressed me greatly.

Then Dr. Frank Kingdon, Master of Ceremonies, called on the several hundred guests present to do their utmost in supporting the campaign for President Roosevelt.

All present were asked to volunteer and call out the amount they wished to give. One man started by announcing one thousand dollars. Several others contributed one thousand dollars and about the fourth name lowered the amount to five hundred dollars.

At this point I was boiling mad. The impact of Mr. Wallace's speech had aroused me to an extremely high pitch. I had started from my office expecting to give nothing, I now felt I would contribute one thousand dollars.

Knowing the men who had made their announcements to be millionaires while I was far from being one, I was disappointed in the way the fund raising job was going.

Spontaneously I almost ran from my chair in the rear of the room to the dais where I asked Dr. Kingdon to please let me make a few remarks. "The speech making is over," he told me. "But, Dr. Kingdon, I am certain I can help raise the standard of giving—" He cut me short and exhibited his impatience with me further by repeating, "The speech making is over!"

"Dr. Kingdon, I will contribute one thousand dollars for every minute I talk." I pleaded with him. And again, more sternly and obviously showing his annoyance with me he reiterated, "Get away PLEASE, the speech making is over."

Now, however, I saw the hand of Sidney Hillman tug at Dr. Kingdon's elbow and he said, "Frank, let the gentleman talk for an hour or two."

I felt inspired and used as my theme "Meeting the Test." I started by reference to Abraham when he met the test by being ready to slay his son Isaac as an offering to God. I referred to how Washington and his men were tested at Valley Forge—the British at Dunkirk, and how in every generation men were called on to "meet the test." I pointed out that this was no ordinary campaign but a crusade against Hitlerism.

In any case I was told I spoke for seven minutes and I wrote out a check for seven thousand dollars.

I had the satisfaction of knowing that my talk helped considerably in the raising of funds that afternoon and at many other meetings in the campaign where the whole incident of seven thousand dollars for seven minutes privilege of speaking was referred to.

Too few realize that one is negligent of his duties as an American if he fails to give of his time, money and ingenuity toward helping the worthy to win elections. When I look back over the years I feel I made one of the best investments of my life in the crusade to vanquish Hitlerism.

HENRY FORD

## *Public Enemy Number One of One World*

Henry Ford II, present head of Ford Motors, is in my opinion a wonderful human being. In my book they do not come any finer.

In the mid-forties he took over the operation of the company when it was on the verge of going broke. In the history of commerce there probably has never been anything to compare with the fabulous comeback young Henry brought about in the Ford Motor Company. In less than fifteen years the company has made billions of dollars, most of which accrues to the great Ford Foundation.

Young Ford cleaned house. He got rid of the treacherous villain so close to his grandfather and countless other cronies whom he knew influenced the founder of the company negatively. He brought in Mr. Breech and other vital, capable men of integrity. He performed a veritable miracle in converting what appeared as a dead outfit into the sparkling, dynamic, worthy competitor of General Motors.

In 1944 I wrote a piece about the grandfather of the present Henry II. I had withheld its publication because of the great respect I have for the grandsons. I have decided to include it in my book because of its historical importance and because I believe the present Fords have the maturity to appreciate that the publication of such monumental truth can only be of value to the world. For as someone great has said, "Only the truth will set us free."

In 1944 a good friend said to me, "If you say a negative word about Henry Ford I will never want to see you again." It infuriated me to see what hate propaganda administered by high sources could do to my beloved friend and I began to look into the situation in depth. I was convinced that Henry Ford did more than any human being in our time to make hate respectable and Detroit the hate capital of America. I then wrote this piece which I believe will make my readers more objective in appraising eminent tycoons.

## PUBLIC ENEMY NO. 1 OF ONE WORLD

*His Name Is.......* *Henry Ford.*
*He Lives In........* *Hate Capital of America (Detroit) Michigan.*
*His Occupation......* *Presently making war implements, but normally making automobiles.*
*His Avocation.......* *Making hate respectable all over the world.*

*God-fearing people charge Henry Ford with the crime of exacting from mankind at least one hundred years of advancement towards love and brotherhood as a price for advancing transportation by a dozen years.*

*My readers and I see him standing by the pearly gates of heaven seeking to gain admittance. He is confronted by that eternal prosecutor, Saint Peter. We now hear him order Henry to sit down on that "hot seat" called TRUTH on which every person on earth will some day be invited to sit.*

ST. PETER: *Fancy you coming up here!*

HENRY: *Why—I've been a good man.*

ST. PETER: *So you say, but our records have it that you are one of the worst hypocrites known to mankind.*

HENRY: *There must be some mistake! Everyone on earth knows Hitler is the one who is responsible for the living hell the people have undergone these past years.*

ST. PETER: *Not being exposed to false gods we are never mistaken in identifying the "higher ups," the men behind the men who pull the trigger.*

HENRY: *I don't understand. I'm a gentle soul. Didn't you ever hear my radio programs? Sweet music—old-fashioned village stuff?*

ST. PETER: *Don't insult our intelligence as you have done to the many millions on earth. What about your dissemination of the Protocols of Zion and the publishing of the Dearborn Independent?*

HENRY: *Oh, that? But that was so long ago, and didn't you hear about my apology to the Jews?*

ST. PETER: *You are contemptible! I must warn you that you are squirming on that TRUTH seat because you hesitate to make a candid confession.*

HENRY: *Already I find this seat cooler since I have resolved to understand myself. I see how misinformed I've been all these years.*

ST. PETER: *Speak the truth!*

HENRY: *By God, I swear I didn't mean to be the number*

*one contributor to the second world war. I was mixed up.*

ST. PETER: *Well, how does that differ from Hitler, Coughlin or the poor devil that killed a policeman when trying to escape from the scene of his crime? They're all mixed up. All evil is the result of people being confused, which begets fear and which in turn begets hate. Do you understand?*

HENRY: *Of course I do! By giving the people cheap transportation I became the richest man on earth. I had reached the highest rung on the SUCCESS LADDER. During the first world war I became so impressed with myself that I proposed to go to Europe and establish peace. I was proud and arrogant with the result that my mission failed and I was the laughing stock of the world. It hurt me to the quick.*

*In this awful position the idea came to me as it has to all evil men since Abraham discovered God: Make a scapegoat of the Jews. Blame them for everything and I would kill two birds with one stone. I would get the public to forget the fool that I really was and establish myself as the fearless prophet of the gentiles.*

*(Newshawks in early 1920's were shouting in all the cities of America, "Read Henry Ford's Dearborn Independent and learn all about the Jews who are the cause of all our troubles.")*

ST. PETER: *Didn't you ever read George Washington's letter to the Jews in Newport, Rhode Island in 1790 in which he said:*

*"For happily the Government of the United States, which gives to bigotry no sanction, to persecution no assistance requires only that they who live under its protection should deem themselves as good citizens, in giving it on all occasions their effectual support.*

*"May the children of the stock of Abraham, who dwell in this land, continue to merit and enjoy the good*

*will of the other inhabitants; while every one shall sit in safety under his own vine and fig-tree, and there shall be none to make him afraid. May the Father of all mercies scatter light and not darkness in our paths, and make us all in our several vocations useful here, and in his own due time and way everlastingly happy."*

HENRY: *No, I didn't read history; in fact, that was my trouble. I shot off my mouth all the time without making sure of my facts. That is why I made a big fool of myself in court. I looked silly when the lawyer for the defense proved that I couldn't answer any historical question correctly.*

ST. PETER: *Well, why didn't you repent?*

HENRY: *The trouble, sir, was that I was surrounded by the wrong kind of people. They hated labor, foreigners, Negroes, Jews and loved only money and power. That is why they hired labor spies in my factories and flattered me into thinking that I was bigger than the government when N.R.A. came along. They sure did a lot to get me mixed up.*

ST. PETER: *Too bad you didn't realize that God was the only source which men must seek for their guide and comfort.*

HENRY: *You said it! I got so mixed up that I began to revel in the fact that a simpleton like me could create a new capital in America. I had a grudge against the Money Capital (Wall Street) and the people's Capital in Washington, so when apostles and ambassadors of hate started to flock to Detroit I felt all hopped up. In recognition for my genius in bringing this about, the trigger man of hate in Berlin, friend Adolf, honored me by sending Fritz Kuhn to cooperate with me. He organized the German American Bund and tried to become the American Fuehrer. Now, in addition to Ford and automobiles, the world came to recognize Detroit as the "Hate Capital" of America.*

ST. PETER: *Weren't you alarmed by this trend of events?*

HENRY: *On the contrary—I had great satisfaction when I received the highest possible recognition from Adolf Hitler in the form of a medal. I was only one of three Americans to receive this coveted award. Lindbergh, the great hero, Watson, the great business machine tycoon (I understand he repented and returned it) and I, the world's greatest industrialist.*

ST. PETER: *Didn't you realize you were trading your birthright to the Cross for the swastika when you accepted that medal?*

HENRY: *I didn't realize anything! I was on a merry-go-round.*

ST. PETER: *Your world was spinning on a politic rather than a prophetic base. Hardly a man in the world has guts enough to fight evil until they personally are affected.*

HENRY: *I now see it clearly. Putting my faith in men instead of God explains my downfall.*

ST. PETER: *Then you see the result of your setting yourself up as the prophet of ignorance?*

HENRY: *Of course, my misdeeds gave courage to the Thyssens and Krupps abroad, to the appeasers and quislings everywhere, and to the isolationists at home. Had I seen God when I reached the top of the SUCCESS LADDER, the world might never have known a Hitler, a Father Coughlin or a Gerald Smith who could point to the fact that the most successful man in the world was a champion of hate.*

ST. PETER: *Did you know that even now down in Argentina they are making full use of your hate propaganda? Whenever a country turns to Fascism there you will find Henry Ford's poison taking front rank in effectively confusing the mind of the common man.*

HENRY: *I know that mankind has been set back at least one hundred years because of my being a monkey instead of a man.*

ST. PETER: *Acknowledge your guilt.*

HENRY: *The second world war represents a clash of two ideologies. God versus the devil. I acknowledge that I have been on the side of the devil, on the side of hate, on the side of power, wealth and prejudice.*

ST. PETER: *Arise from the TRUTH seat. Walk over to the devil's chute. I consign you to hell.*

HENRY: *God! Have mercy on my soul!*

To the credit of Henry Ford let it be said that he left a Foundation which is the greatest force for good that any family has ever had.

I therefore pray to God that he forgive the old rascal and transfer him from hell to heaven.

LEGISLATION SHOULD PRECEDE EDUCATION

## *How Shall We Deal With Hate?*

Why don't we follow God's example and legislate before we educate? God gave Moses the Ten Commandments at Mount Sinai. He did not prescribe an educational program to teach people why it was wrong to steal, to kill, to bear false witness. He said, "Thou shalt not steal." And it became the law of the Israelites there and then. Then Moses and his followers realized that leaders ever after had the obligation to educate their followers on the wisdom of the law.

Thousands of years have passed since Sinai and people still break the Commandments. Imagine how many times more wickedness would prevail if legislation were to be held in abeyance until education had done the job of obliterating bad behavior.

Consider a suburban community where many accidents have occurred on a certain corner. Numerous children were injured and one was killed. The community is up in arms. Meetings are held in churches and schools. Talk, talk, talk all intended to educate. Wouldn't it be wiser to legislate first? How? Simply by having a green and red stop light placed on the corner.

My thoughts are concerned with hate . . . the propagation and dissemination of hate literature and all other hate propaganda. Jesus and others centuries before him preached love of neighbor, yet thousands of years later there is more hate in the hearts of people than ever before. Did not President Kennedy's assassination prove to what extent hate exists in our country when so many applauded the insane act? I doubt that wholesale stealing can do a country nearly as much harm as wholesale hating.

If one must hate why not confine it to the boundaries of one's own home? If one wants to teach hate to his children let him do it in his home. We, however, must through legislation make these sick minded people aware of the fact that they break the law and are subject to fine and punishment if they preach hatred to others.

I have supported the Civil Liberties Union, the League for Industrial Democracy, the U.D.A. and the Americans for Democratic Action and most liberal organizations. Roger Baldwin, Freda Kirchwey and Morris Ernst and all others in the forefront of civil liberties and free speech know I champion their causes. Nevertheless I do not believe free speech entitles one to preach hatred of an individual or a group. By all means let hatred be preached of unrighteousness, injustice, poverty, disease and all other evils. Let there be hatred of evil, but not of human beings.

If from the time of Leviticus who centuries before

Jesus said, "Love thy neighbor," laws were on the statute books making it a crime to hate human beings there might have been a happier history to record.

How ridiculous can a nation be when after Hitler we permit freedom of speech to a group wearing the swastika and calling themselves American Nazis? Justice Oliver Wendell Holmes made it plain that free speech does not entitle one to yell "fire" in a crowded theater.

"As a dog who returneth to his vomit so are those who repeateth their folly." Haven't men permitted the repetition of murder and massacre to go on generation after generation?

I appeal to the heart and conscience of our lawmakers to pass a law that makes it a criminal offense for one to preach hatred for any human being or group of persons.

Let's follow God's example in His creation of the universe. Let us legislate first and educate forever after.

A ONE MAN CAMPAIGN FOR ROOSEVELT

## *I Am Invited to the White House*

After my $7000.00 initiation fee, I was very active until the eve of the election.

My office was virtually converted into a special headquarters for Roosevelt. I paid little attention to the dress business and gave almost all my time to the campaign.

Above all else I regarded this as my personal crusade against Hitler. Our armed forces had already performed miracles in landing in North Africa, Italy and France. Once entrenched, they piled victory on top of victory and were smashing the Nazi forces. Hitlerism was doomed except for the fact that a defeat for Roosevelt might have meant that another president would make some kind of a deal with Hitler short of unconditional surrender. I would have worked for the devil himself to prevent a Roosevelt defeat and in a sense I did just that only a few weeks before the November election.

I conceived of a plan which, I was told, brought the clergy actively into the campaign for the first time in American history. A magazine called the *Protestant Digest* was published by a man named Kenneth Leslie. I knew him to be anti-Catholic and felt certain he was a Communist. It was distasteful for me to do business with him, but as I said, I would trade with the devil himself in order to defeat Hitler. I succeeded in getting Leslie to procure the signatures of Bishop J. D. Humphrey and fifteen other Protestant clergymen to endorse a piece in which Leslie and I collaborated for a political advertisement headlined by the phrase—"Be not deceived—"

"BE NOT DECEIVED . . ."

*As clergymen who may take no direct part in a political campaign, our deep concern with ethical and spiritual values leads us to denounce the current unethical and undignified appeals of Dewey supporters which are being made with or without the knowledge of Thomas E. Dewey.*

*We make particular reference to the following:*

One—*The sordid and irreverent play upon the sacred emotions of mothers, wives and sweethearts with deceptive spot radio appeals such as "To get the boys home sooner, vote for Dewey."*

Two—*The insinuations by Dewey supporters, among them Vice-Presidential candidate Bricker, that the President is a Hillman prisoner, and the un-American references to Hillman's foreign birth and the ridiculing of his former occupation as a clothing worker.*

Three—*The numerous attempts in Hitler fashion to make it appear that Communism is a threat to the United States, when in reality America is genuinely endangered by innumerable reactionary, isolationist, anti-Semitic, pro-Fascist groups.*

Four—*The base appeal to the self-interest of individuals who are resentful of the adjustments they have had to make to the demands of war, and the attempt to place the blame for the necessity of adjustments in the wrong place.*

Five—*The implied threat of Dewey himself in his speech of October 25th that the Congress will sabotage the peace unless he is made President.*

Six—*The attempts by numerous Dewey supporting groups to win votes by fomenting and exploiting race prejudice.*

*This kind of propaganda is all too reminiscent of tactics employed in Germany. We protest against this duplication of Nazi strategy in the United States. We, members of the clergy, representing various Christian denominations, call upon our fellow-Christians everywhere to join us in our repudiation of the above-named tactics.*

It cost me eighteen thousand dollars to have this advertisement placed in leading papers from the *New York Times* in the East to the *San Francisco Chronicle* on the West Coast. The ad appeared only a few days before the election.

I also supported the Democratic National Committee, the Independents for Roosevelt, the Republicans for Roosevelt and Businessmen for Roosevelt.

The reader will recall that I had never been active in a political campaign before. I had grudgingly decided I would contribute one hundred dollars when Mr. Hoffman told me it was the thing to do on our way down to listen to Wallace. However, when election eve rolled around my contributions amounted to seven thousand dollars for the seven minute talk, eighteen thousand dollars to have the clergymen's message brought to the people all over America, and thousands more to the various F.D.R. groups—a grand total exceeding thirty thousand dollars.

A powerful personage said that had I given the money to the Democratic National Committee I could have had an ambassadorship. I told him if an ambassadorship was what I wanted I should have done exactly that, but I wanted to do all in my power to make certain Hitler's unconditional surrender would be unconditional.

However, I did get an invitation from the White House to meet the President on October 19, 1944. There were forty of us invited to that particular event. I distinctly remember Frederic March and his wife, Florence Eldridge. I was directly behind Bette Davis in the line that marched toward the President seated in his wheel chair. As we approached, Ed Pauley, Treasurer of the Democratic National Committee, introduced each of us to the President.

A delightful buffet luncheon was served with the President's daughter acting as hostess. I sat at a small table with James Tobin, head of the powerful teamster's Union, and Eddie Albert, the beloved actor.

The next day I sent the following letter to the President:

*October 20, 1944*

*President Franklin Delano Roosevelt*
*The White House*
*Washington, D.C.*

*Dear Mr. President:*

*Humbly we came, proudly we saw and confidently we left the White House late Thursday afternoon.*

*Humble, because a liberal America makes possible the invitation of the President of the United States even to foreign born citizens whom you recognize on the same level as those descended from Mayflower stock.*

*Proud, because we know that providence has brought us to the house where dwells the greatest symbol of humanity in the world. Even your enemies know that Franklin and Eleanor Roosevelt are the torch bearers of love, freedom and hope for all mankind.*

*Confident, because the twinkle in your bright, clear eyes exuded the plain fact that with God's aid you would lead us to victory against the Axis abroad and against reaction at home, so that the people could go ahead with the business of establishing the brotherhood of man.*

*The strength and warmth of your handshake, your radiant smile and vigorous expression give the lie to the enemies of the people who know they can "handle" a young man but fear your strength and magnetic spiritual dynamism.*

*Indeed, it was a rare privilege to have met you.*

*You must take comfort in knowing that the overwhelming majority of mankind give you their hearts and minds in recognition of your great service to their God.*

*Sincerely yours,*

JEWS

## *Brothers Not Burdens*

Considering that they represent only one half of one per cent of the world's population, do you know of any other people about whom so much has been said and written as the Jews?

Yet there are not many, including Jews themselves,

who can tell you whether they are a people, a race, a nation or merely a religion.

As for me, I know only what I feel and this is that we are a large family or what the Scots would call a clan. I feel related to every Jew on earth. When I hear bad about them I worry and often have wept. When I hear good I rejoice as if it were about a brother.

When I read of a Jew committing a crime I cringe, I shrivel up and feel ashamed. When I read about Admiral Rickover, Dr. Jonas Salk, Sandy Koufax and of the thousands from the time of Ezekiel to Einstein, my heart swells with pride.

Is a Texan less an American because of the fierce pride he has for his native state? Is the Italian to be condemned as an American for the pride he takes in accomplishments of Italy? So do I glory and revel in the accomplishments of my people in the tiny State of Israel. I meet Jews who are indifferent to the plight of persecuted and homeless Jews. Other Jews say they are tired of giving. One said to me, "Sam, don't you think it a burden to be expected to support our people indefinitely?"

I told him my favorite Lincoln story. When Lincoln was a circuit judge he was riding in a carriage up a steep hill in a downpour of rain. Midway to the top of the hill he noticed a colored boy about twelve years old carrying a little pickaninny on his back. Lincoln yelled out, "Come in, Son, let me help you with your burden." With no hesitation the boy fired back, "Look heah, Mistah, dis ain't no burden . . . dis am mah brother."

That colored boy spoke for me. Jews in trouble and in need are not my burden. They are my brothers.

A VISIT FROM HENRY BERNSTEIN

## *Why I Became a Millionaire*

Early in February 1946 I had a visit from Mr. Henry Bernstein, the executive director of New York's United Jewish Appeal. I was in the midst of writing this book when he visited me at my Florida home.

He lost no time in telling me why he wished to see me. He explained that the liberation of Hitler's victims from concentration camps necessitated transporting them to other lands, particularly to Palestine. It was to be the greatest life saving endeavor in the history of private philanthropy. The United Jewish Appeal needed one hundred million dollars to do the job.

To raise this stupendous amount they were going to make it clear to the prospects that the gift in 1946 was to be a ONE TIME GIFT and that in the year following one could go back to one's normal pattern of giving.

He told me he was not flattering me in saying I was the first Jew in America to be contacted for a contribution. He gave as the reason the fact that before calling on the gigantic lead-off contributors he hoped to be inspired and stimulated by my gift.

I asked him to tell me what gift from me would meet his expectations. He said, "Fifteen thousand dollars would be dramatic and wonderful." When I told him I would make it twenty-five thousand dollars, he jumped up from his seat and shouted, "Man—that does it! This gives me just the 'shot in the arm' I need to start the campaign. Now I can tell our leaders about a small unknown garment maker giving eight times his 1945 gift."

When Henry left I began to think about all that had

transpired in the past several years and how we were praying for the day when Hitler's victims could be saved. I visualized hundreds of thousands of emaciated skeletons who were formerly human beings as you and I, now dependent on our mercy.

Thinking along these lines and considering my recent recovery from a heart attack I made up my mind that if this was to be a ONE TIME GIFT I would go all out and give twenty-five per cent of my entire net worth to the 1946 campaign. I went to the telephone and called Mr. Bernstein at the Sovereign Hotel and told him I would contribute fifty thousand dollars. He was overwhelmed and said my gift virtually insured the campaign's success.

Having appeased my gnawing conscience I could settle down again to writing my life story. I was doing nicely until one night my sleep was disturbed. I thought of how I would hurt the 1947 campaign when I went back to normal giving. People would forget the sacrifice made in going from three thousand dollars in 1945 to fifty thousand dollars in 1946. When I would go back again to three thousand dollars there would be too many who might cut drastically but who never raised much in 1946. It occurred to me that to serve Hitler's victims best I should endeavor to go all out in expanding my business to be able to give more to the United Jewish Appeal.

I flew to New York early in March. I told my associates that while I did not take myself seriously, I felt it was incumbent upon me to use all my ingenuity and resources to grow in business and to make more money. This was a complete reversal of my instructions when I left New York in December shortly after recovering from my heart attack.

They knew this ambition did not emanate from a need for better living but rather my desire for better giving.

There was still nine months left in the year for us to roll up our sleeves and see how far we could go on our capital and ideas. I promised to supply the ideas but counted on them to execute my plans.

So it happened that several months later I came up with a revolutionary idea of selling our product by mail direct to the consumer under the name of Florida Fashions. When 1946 ended we had doubled our 1945 volume and more than trebled our profits. Thus in 1947 I was able to give United Jewish Appeal seventy-five thousand dollars and in 1948 I wrote out a single check for one hundred thousand dollars to help save hundreds of thousands of lives and create a haven and a homeland in Israel.

With God's aid I have made several million dollars since then. I determined to become rich in order to help Hitler's victims. I never changed my style of living. One respected Jewish leader, addressing a large gathering in New York, said about me without mentioning my name, "In this very room there is a man who lives like a pauper and gives like a prince."

In 1952, on my fiftieth birthday, Henry Montor, who was National Head of United Jewish Appeal since its inception and then headed the sale of State of Israel Bonds from the beginning, wrote a congratulatory note saying, "You more than any man in America established the principle that we owe a tithe of our possessions to our brothers. You projected on the national scene the idea that 'my goods are my peoples.' "

God knows that I did not seek recognition but I received it in abundance. My business grew to become the largest producer of women's and children's dresses in America. Many attributed my rise to the doing of good deeds. I would tell them that the God I believe in did not pay dividends in health or wealth. The one and only thing one could be sure to obtain from God for doing good is a free and easy conscience.

Why did I become a millionaire?

Because I wanted to match the greatest need with the greatest deed.

Because I wanted to set an unheard of standard of giving to inspire others. To achieve this I had to make as much money as possible.

$90 AND AN IDEA

## *The Rise and Fall of Florida Fashions*

My mind was concentrating on ways and means of enlarging our business. I was determined to do all possible to make a lot of money.

An idea came to me which was to make it possible for me to earn more money faster than anyone in the dress business. It came about in this way. We were invited to Sanford, Florida by the Shames' when their child Jimmy was born. I was seated on a platform holding the baby as the doctor circumcized him. The nurse removed the infant from my arms and at that moment the big idea entered my mind.

Approaching the father of the child I said to him, "Frank, how do you like the name 'Florida Fashions'?" He said that it sounded good to him. "In that case," I said, "we are going into the mail order business. You have the Florida address, I have 1700 dozen dresses of one style I can't get rid of. I'll run a $90 ad in the *New York News* and we'll keep our fingers crossed."

The ad pulled well and encouraged us to try many others in newspapers in other cities. We sold the 20,400 dresses @2 for $5, whereas the best offer I had had was only 75¢ each. The dresses were made in 64×60 percale for $25.50 a dozen. With the ending of the war 80×80 percale was coming into plentiful supply. The buyers simply wouldn't touch anything made of 64×60 even at the reduced price of $15 a dozen. I was stuck with over 20,000 dresses unless I was willing to let them go so that the buyer could retail them for $1 or $1.19. This I was reluctant to do. The mail order idea bailed me out and big things were in store for us.

Florida Fashions, Sanford, Florida had come into being. I then lent Frank Shames $25,000 and I put up a like amount; so with $50,000 we started in earnest to sell dresses by mail direct to the consumer.

From tiny $90 ads we graduated to running half page and finally full page ads. Some succeeded while others flopped. It was like a seesaw . . . our affairs went up and down, but we emerged with fair profits during 1946–'47–'48. My giving to the United Jewish Appeal went from $3,000 in 1945, $50,000 in 1946, $75,000 in 1947 and imagine my satisfaction when in 1948 I wrote out a single check for $100,000 to help Hitler's victims.

In late 1949 I took over Frank Shames' interest in Florida Fashions and paid him out several hundred thousand dollars. He was capable, conscientious and the soul of integrity. He managed our affairs very well. My severance with Frank as my partner was due to the fact that we saw that the only profit that could be derived in Florida Fashions was to the manufacturer. Hence, Florida Fashions was, until the time of its liquidation in 1962, to serve strictly as an outlet for the merchandise my factories produced.

The original small ads ceased to pull; larger black and white ads no longer brought results. An occasional full page ad did well, but now we discovered full page color ads. They were expensive. In the *Chicago Tribune* the cost was about $5,000. In the *New York Daily News* over $10,000 and in Hearst's *American Weekly* we paid over $20,000 for a single page in color.

We saw that in a short time the color ads too would flop and that our future lay only in putting out catalogs. In any case, we decided in 1950 to be unconcerned about profits but had only one objective. Advertise to the limit in color ads so as to obtain the names for a mailing list to whom we would send catalogs.

In 1950 we spent almost $1,500,000 for advertising. In all history no garment firm to date had spent anywhere near that sum in a single year.

Late that year with several million fresh names in our files we issued our first tiny catalog. We had fair success. Then we began mailing six, seven and even eight catalogs a year. That would total over 25,000,000 catalogs during the year.

At the time this was happening the war in Korea began. We were renting about six small buildings from the U.S. Navy. Now they gave us notice that they were going to reactivate the base at Sanford and gave us ninety days to move.

It's an "ill wind" that blows no good. This request from the navy turned out to be a good thing for us. We were limited in the help we could get in Sanford. Now the industrial Commission in nearby Orlando, only 17 miles away, provided a site for us and in less than 90 days we were operating in a 54,000 square foot plant. It was on Colonial Avenue, the main artery cutting across the state from Tampa to Cape Canaveral (changed to Kennedy.)

The Orlando Industrial Commission paid $2,000 an acre for the thirteen acres on which we built our plant. They turned it over to us for only $1,000 providing we kept three hundred or more people employed steadily for a period of five years. In 1955 they turned the deed over to us. The land given to us for $1,000 was now worth over $100,000. When I sold it in 1963 I received $200,000 for it . . . 200 times the original cost. (The building brought $150,000 additional.)

In all my life I never made money in investments in stocks or real estate. Always I lost what added up to a princely sum. The lucky break of getting 200 times every dollar invested in the Orlando tract was enough to keep me from ever complaining thereafter.

We developed the most successful mail order firm specializing in low priced apparel for women and children. Our sales volume reached $13,000,000 with over 4,000,000 customers names in our files. We had customers in every area in the United States where a post office existed.

In the early fifties three extraordinary powerful movements emerged on a giant scale:

a. Credit
b. Shopping Centers
c. Discount Houses

The giant mail order firm Spiegels promoted credit as never before in that field. Sears, Montgomery Ward, Aldens and Bellas Hess too began to play up credit on a gigantic scale. Hundreds of other retailers large and small committed to selling only for cash were forced to revise their policies. Soon the giants J. C. Penney, W. T. Grant and numerous others initiated credit.

Florida Fashions could not afford to introduce credit. Specializing only in low priced apparel the average sale was only about $5 . . . far too little for a credit operation. In the big general mail order firms the average sales ticket included thousands of items and particularly high priced sales such as refrigerators, washing machines, television sets and everything for the farm and home.

Overnight, so to speak, from coast to coast there sprang up shopping centers and discount stores. This affected

Florida Fashions in this way. Whereas hundreds of thousands of its customers worked for a living and found it difficult if possible to shop in stores, they now were delighted to have the privilege of shopping in stores in the evenings and even on Sundays.

Florida Fashions enabled my basic business, The House of Perfection, to make millions of dollars in manufacturing women's and children's dresses. This made it possible for me to fulfill my dream of setting new standards for giving; to help restore to normalcy the lives of the survivors of the concentration camps and create in Israel a haven for Jews fleeing from tyranny and persecution.

Now in the late fifties we began to feel the nightmarish change in our business. It kept slumping worse each year during '57–'58–'59. We saw the handwriting on the wall. We were doomed to fail. The business that helped make us rich and famous was destined to fold up. We made plans to pay off our creditors and liquidate the company.

The business that made millions for us was to be no more and even worse was responsible for hurting The House of Perfection. Suffice to say we shall always have a soft spot in our hearts for Florida Fashions.

## *I Discuss It With Jennie*

Jennie Grossinger has been my close friend for thirty years. Her resort in the Catskills is probably the most famous Jewish hostelry in the world. I have always considered her to be the female counterpart of myself in that she too has an all consuming lust for learning. I know of no one who has grown and developed as a human being more than my friend Jennie.

At her resort she approached me at the luncheon table to ask what I was writing. I told her of a new interest in which I had become absorbed. I had concluded that every positive quality in a human being had to be complemented with another if it was to have a good result.

I then explained to Jennie that I had read John Steinbeck's *Of Mice and Men.* The central character, Lennie, loved his sweetheart so much that he embraced her too strongly and crushed her to death. I analysed the tragedy and concluded that Lennie was strong and powerful, but he was not tender. Though he adored his sweetheart he killed her without meaning to. Therefore I created this maxim, "It is good to be strong only if one is gentle."

Even among nations it is tragic to find power and strength if the nation is a "bully" such as Nazi Germany. Thank God that a strong America has never had anything but a gentle policy to other nations.

I got started on what to me is a pleasant game. It is fun and philosophical.

Is it good to be handsome or beautiful? Of course, providing that one is also modest.

It is good to be rich only if one is generous to those in need.

It is good to be wise only if one instructs others wisely.

It is good to be clever only if one is honest.

It is good to observe that which is good only if it leads to admiration and emulation.

It is good to have talent only if it serves to please others.

Jennie asked if I would create a maxim that would apply specifically to her. I told her, "It is good to be successful only if one remembers one's humble beginnings."

Take note of the many people who have been favored in so many ways and who are unhappy. This is apparent among celebrities. Consider the many who acquire extraordinary intellects but who are only made snobbish thereby.

To all these I would merely say, "It is good to be gifted only if it inspires one to be of service to others."

I trust the reader too will enjoy playing this philosophical game.

TWO PACIFIC TRANSACTIONS

## *Doing Business on Monday in the Spirit of Sunday*

Textile prices reached an all time high in 1948. Subsequently prices trebled as is illustrated by the fact that Pacific Mills shipped us two hundred thousand yards of percales at forty-five cents a yard, but when they reached us the price hit thirty cents.

On my return from Florida in late spring my buyer told me that luckily the goods from Pacific were crocked (dust particles from the printing remained on the cloth). We were not obliged to accept and would therefore save thirty thousand dollars. We were delighted with this stroke of luck.

Fate—rather the slogan I was committed to, decreed otherwise. An executive of Pacific Mills called to tell me he was waiting for me to return to New York. He said, "Mr. Goldfarb, on the basis of legality we owe your firm thirty thousand dollars. Since you advertise "Do Business on Monday in the Spirit of Sunday" I want you to know that you would be receiving money that morally you were not entitled to." I told him I placed morality above legality and would not accept money just because the law said it was coming to me.

I was then told that if any of the dresses made of the crocked fabric were returned to me they would give me a refund for the full retail price. I accepted. We received so few returns that I didn't even bother to make any claim.

Coincidentally a number of years later Mr. Ed Kelleher, sales manager of Pacific Mills called on me to say that the big brass from the Boston headquarters were in town. He pleaded with me to have lunch with them as he wanted them to hear directly from me why we were doing no business with them.

At the luncheon table besides Mr. Kelleher, were Messrs. Bradley and Singer, the two top vice presidents. I gave them these three reasons: first, they seldom were priced competitively; second, they offered too limited a selection of designs; and last, their service was unsatisfactory. They required three weeks to print fabrics. I sometimes needed merchandise in a week or less and could get it elsewhere.

They told me they would take extraordinary measures to give me better opportunity for design selection and even meet my service requirements. Only price was a stumbling block. I offered to buy one million yards at twenty-eight and a half cents which I told them I was getting percales for at the time. They said they had not sold any under thirty cents, but they would call on the phone at three o'clock to give me the answer.

In the meantime the giant Pacific competitor called to tell me twenty-eight and three quarters cents was the last word on price and I placed a two million yard order. At three o'clock the phone rang again. "Sam," Kelleher shouted, "we are accepting your order for one million yards at twenty-eight and one half cents." Imagine his surprise and consternation when I calmly said, "Ed, change the price to twenty-eight and three-quarters because I erroneously thought I was going to get the lower price, but in fact just closed at the twenty-eight and three-quarter level."

The following morning Mr. Bradley and Mr. Singer accompanied the sales manager in calling on me. They wanted me to know that every employee of their giant company would be told about the man who once presented them with thirty thousand dollars and who yesterday handed them another twenty-five hundred dollars because he had to "do business on Monday in the spirit of Sunday."

A PHONE CALL FROM JACK ALBERT

## *Truth Is Stranger Than Fiction*

It was about three in the afternoon and for the first time in our business career we, the top executives of our company, were sitting in discussion as to where we could borrow two hundred thousand dollars from sources outside our banks. We owed the banks the limit. We didn't want to approach them. If only we could find four friends each of whom could lend us fifty thousand dollars.

I said to my secretary, "Put down these names—Sam Schneirson, Fred Katzner, Sam Hoffman, Larry Lipson—" and at that point I was interrupted by a telephone call.

"You told me not to put any calls through to you, but this man threatened to have you fire me if I didn't, so please forgive me," said the switchboard operator. I said, "Hello" to the presumptuous party who happened to be Jack Albert, an old neighbor from Forest Hills.

"Hello, Sam, and how are you? Getting a bit ritzy not wanting to speak to anyone? Listen, Sam, I am putting you down as a fifty thousand dollar investor which will include nine others for a total of five hundred thousand dollars to open a pipe factory in Israel." I was taken aback by this "little Napoleon" and could not help but consider the ironic coincidence that he was talking about fifty thousand dollars at the very moment we were using that identical denomination for our pressing problem.

"Jack," I replied, "I am in no position to talk to you now—how about calling me next week?"

"Nothing doing," was the reply from the other end, "You're the guy who got me all hopped up about Israel and now you aren't going to make a fool out of me by letting me down. I've told the other fellows that they can count on Sam Goldfarb."

I went on to explain that under no circumstances could I consider his proposition and would he be good enough to excuse me and understand. Whereupon Jack Albert said, "Sam, you sound as if you are disturbed. Do you need money?" I shot back, "Yes, I do." He inquired, "How much?" I told him two hundred thousand dollars and to my utter amazement he nonchalantly remarked, "O.K.

I'll have a check sent over to you in forty-five minutes."

I thought he was joking and said to him, "Look here, Jack, I'm in no mood for humor. Why would you want to lend me two hundred thousand dollars?" "Why not? Aren't we friends?" he inquired. I told him we were not friends and he asked me to explain. I went on to say that friends were those who meet often to dine together, to play golf together, to do things together, and above all, to confide in one another. We, on the other hand, had seldom seen each other in the past twenty years since he had moved away from Forest Hills.

Then he stunned me by saying, "You son of a b——; who else but you would tell someone you're not his friend when he offers to lend you two hundred thousand dollars? Tell me . . . when you get my check, will you then say I'm your friend?" I said, "You know damn well I'll be your friend . . . the very best."

Just before closing we got the check for two hundred thousand dollars. I put it into my wallet. Going home I said to Gene, "Let's have a little fun with Mother."

At the dinner table at a propitious moment, Gene said, "By the way, Dad—remember that gentleman in the pipe business who sat next to us at the United Jewish Appeal luncheon in Miami? Perhaps we can get fifty thousand dollars from him." Frances burst into laughter. "Fifty thousand dollars from Jack Albert the pipe man? He wouldn't lend you five hundred dollars." Then I pulled out the check and showed it to Frances.

One would hardly believe such a story. It was, however, a fact. Proving that sometimes truth is stranger than fiction.

FROM RAGS TO RICHES

## *Some Deny It—Others Take Pride in It*

Why is it that some try to hide the fact that they were born and reared in a poor family while others revel and glory in it?

A wealthy widow, whose deceased husband had been a close friend of mine, brought along her top business executive to dine with us. In the course of conversation I brought up the fact that when she and I were children we played together in the slums of St. Louis. The following day, over the telephone, she reprimanded me for referring to her childhood and extracted a promise from me that never again would I mention her impoverished background.

On the other hand I recall the time I had dinner at the home of Barney Balaban, head of Paramount Films. This man of wealth has spent a fortune buying papers that have great value and importance to our government. Then he presents them as gifts to the country he is so proud to serve. The original manuscript of the Star Spangled Banner by Francis Scott Key is one of the items he purchased.

I saw copies of the various items he gave to the United States of America. In the same beautiful library he proudly shows the pictures of his orthodox Jewish parents and the place of his birth . . . the second floor of a wooden shack, the ground floor of which served as the family grocery store. This was in the heart of Chicago's ghetto.

The mature and integrated man is proud of his humble origin and wants always to be reminded of it, as in the story of King David.

It is said that visiting dignitaries visiting King David invariably asked, "Why is it that all over the world palaces are repositories for trophies won in battle, beautiful jewels, colorful tapestries and other rare phenomena? Your Majesty's walls are adorned only with rams' horns."

King David's simple reply was, "As I sit on my throne, high above the populace, it is easy for me to have my ego inflated. That is why wherever I cast my eyes I want to see rams' horns to remind me that I was once a shepherd."

The smaller the person, the bigger the ego; the bigger the person, the more humble and grateful he is.

LEON AND FREDA

## *The Long and Short of Perfection*

I have had good luck in developing young people into top executives. I'm going to tell you about a pair . . . a young man and woman who for many years were called "The Long and Short of Perfection." (The name of my company is Perfection.)

Leon Gold is six feet three and Freda Bookay is less than five feet tall. Both were twenty years of age when they came to work for me. They are known, respected and loved by everyone in our industry and especially by buyers from coast to coast. In addition to personality and ability, they possess integrity to a degree that is uncommon in any field of endeavor, as is illustrated by this remarkable story.

Because of a serious arterial condition I developed early in 1942, I depended on them to run my business. I supplied the ideas from Florida or wherever I might be and they executed them.

From 1942 through 1957 when Freda retired, they lunched together almost every day. They were as close and friendly as it was possible for two business associates to be. They lent dignity to their positions and inspired all who came in contact with them. Their earnings were in substantial five figures.

In 1950 I made Leon President and Freda, Executive Vice-President. I moved up to Chairman of the Board. I was surprised at their lack of enthusiasm. Leon especially evidenced no satisfaction, and for several days actually appeared unhappy.

On the fourth day the mystery was cleared for me. Returning from their daily luncheon, Freda, The Short One, excitedly came into my office and said, "Listen to this. I could no longer contain myself witnessing Leon appearing so morose and plainly asked him to explain. Guess what the big Palooka said to me? He hadn't slept a wink for several nights. His digestion is terrible and he has been most unhappy with the Presidency. Why? Here's his answer, 'Because I feel Sam made a mistake. He should have made you President.' And what do you think I said when I heard that?" Freda exclaimed. "I said 'Leon, up to this minute I felt the same way as you. I felt that because of my being tiny and wearing skirts the boss discriminated in your favor, but hearing you say what you did, I now agree with Sam. Anyone with such super integrity added to your other qualities is the proper man for the spot.' "

Now that The Tall One got off his chest what was bothering him and the understanding from The Short One so instantaneously, all turned bright for him, for her and for our business.

MY BIGGEST MISTAKE

## *How I Made My First Million Dollars*

I believe that in 1948 America witnessed the greatest inflation year in its history. In most cases textiles were selling at four times the price at which they sold only eight years earlier.

The most popular fabrics used for ladies' house dresses are percales and particularly one construction called eighty square (80×80) because of its being so smooth and sturdy and having eighty threads to the inch each way. In 1940 I paid 10¢ a yard for it. In 1948 the cost skyrocketed to 45¢. I sought to avoid paying this outrageous price.

An idea came to my mind as one day I read the quotations for cotton greige goods in the *Daily News Record.* I noticed a certain fabric called sheeting in a construction which before the war sold at a slightly higher price than eighty squares but which I now saw listed at 5¢ a yard less than 80×80. Being impetuous, I plunged and bought 2,000,000 yards.

The four styles I developed in house dresses sizes 12 to 52 were turned down by the buyers. They felt sheeting was too coarse for house dresses and preferred paying the higher price for dresses made of the lovely-feeling eighty squares.

There I was, stuck with a three quarters of a million dollar purchase and the laughing stock of the industry. I didn't know which way to turn. The most promising profit year for all looked bleak for me. Still, there were ten months left in the year, and God inspired me with an idea.

It occurred to me that house dress buyers and consumers were especially fabric-conscious. They would feel the fabric while they glanced at the style of the dress. The young girls who bought junior sizes, however, cared little about fabric but were overwhelmingly interested in the style, the pattern of the print, and the coloring. Junior size dresses 9 to 15, however, were not sold in the stores below $5.98 retail.

So—what did I do? I developed a group of junior styles which I labelled DOTTIE DARLIN. I saved about one-third the yardage, and instead of $25.50 for the house-dresses I priced the juniors at $42.00 a dozen. Now with a tremendously higher profit margin I could afford to give the department stores a large advertising allowance. We then sold leading stores in the large cities on condition they run a full-page ad in color promoting DOTTIE DARLIN Juniors at $5.98.

The results were gratifying. DOTTIE DARLIN sold like hot cakes and we converted what loomed up as a dark loss into a bright, sunny million-dollar profit year.

## HIS WORD WAS AS GOOD AS HIS BOND

### *That Explains My $100,000 Purchase*

The largest manufacturer of underwear in the United States had a plant for sale in Columbia, South Carolina. We were badly in need of a southern plant. Their New York office was in the same building as ours. I met their president, Sam Schneirson with whom I had been friendly through joint interests in communal affairs.

I asked Mr. Schneirson to explain why they were selling the plant and what he would take for it. He told me the only reason for selling was their decision not to expand further at the time. They had just bought the plant, thought it to be first rate, had no fault of any kind to find with it. As for the price, Sam said, "One hundred thousand dollars is what I was determined to get, but in your case I would accept seventy-five thousand dollars." I said, "Okay, you have made a sale." He replied, "I won't sell you the plant unless you and your associates go down and inspect it." I explained to him why that was unnecessary, saying, "I am ignorant about the manufacturing end of our business. I have no one connected with me whose judgment I respect as much as that of your production chief and yourself. As long as you say the plant is all right, you have rendered me a service and I am grateful."

We shook hands to close the deal. As I was about to leave Mr. Schneirson told me they would be leaving their offices on Broadway and move to Fifth Avenue in about four months. Would I be interested in taking it over completely? "How much?" I inquired. "Twenty-five thousand dollars," was his answer. Jocularly I replied, "Okay, McNeil, it's a deal." And there hangs the tale of a one hundred thousand dollar purchase made in a matter of minutes without any checking. Our attorneys closed the deal officially a few days later.

Is that the way I conducted my business? No! As a rule we were scrupulously careful in making purchases. In this particular instance I was dealing with a man whose reputation for honesty and integrity was second to none in the mercantile world. The word of Sam Schneirson was as good as his bond.

Time corroborated my judgment. Since 1950 we have

operated that plant. It has always been good, but today it is better than ever.

THE WHOLE WORLD SHOULD KNOW

## *The Wonderful Italians*

I made a wish in a gondola in Venice back in 1949. It was during their gala summer spectacle. They had a display of elaborate electrically lighted floats. They were colorfully decorated as only the Italians are capable of doing. There was music in the air. There was dancing on the brilliantly exotic boats as they sailed smoothly down the Grand Canal. We sat in our gondola for hours just to witness the grandiose affair. We were with Rabbi Jonah Wise and his wife, Mr. and Mrs. Abraham Krasne, and the young rabbi of Venice.

I wished that I could let the whole world know how wonderful the Italian people were to the Jews during the partnership of Mussolini with Hitler. As we enjoyed the spectacle, the rabbi told us stories of the extraordinary heroism of the populace. Behind the iron bars on the square in the Jewish Quarter of Venice the rabbi could look out and see police and army officers assaulted by Italians. They weren't college professors, journalists, or prominent in any field. They were ordinary people who toiled endlessly to make a living. Housewives would double up their fists and walk up to an officer shouting as they pounded him, "Leave them alone—free them—they are every bit as good as you."

The rabbi told us that he heard similar stories from other rabbis in Italy. The people were openly defiant of the authorities and even foolhardy in risking their lives because of their righteous indignation of what was being done to their Jewish neighbors. Of course after the war, the whole world learned of the thousands of Jewish lives that were saved by the Pope hiding them in the Vatican.

The world knew, too, that the Italian people hated the alliance with Hitler. Their hearts were rarely with the Nazis in their opposition to America and their allies. The soldiers in battle didn't have the spirit to fight against those with whom they wished they were in partnership. Even Mussolini's daughter, Edda, exhibited the warmth, the decency, the humanity and the civilization of the Italian people. In the postwar book "*I Was Hitler's Interpreter*," the author, Schmidt, reveals that on the several times Edda Ciano visited Hitler it was only for the purpose of begging him to be decent to the Jews.

One story above the many others I heard proves conclusively the true spirit of the Italians during their ordeal of a Hitler alliance.

A Jewish girl, employed as a clerk in a small shop, was being hidden in the attic of her employer's home. This was in Milan at the height of the Nazis' search for Jews to be captured and put to death in the crematoria. After many months she could not endure her stay in the attic. She persuaded her employer that she would lose her mind unless she went to work. One day as she was going home she had the scare of her life. She was a moment away from being detected by the murderers. She was seated on one of those streetcars that are hitched on to another in front. Two Nazis got on the first car and began asking the passengers to show their "papers." The Jewess had none and was beside herself in fear of certain death. Luckily, she had the presence of mind to appeal to a black shirted Fascist army captain seated opposite her. She seized a moment when the Nazis were looking at "papers" to dash across the aisle, seat herself next to the captain and tell him of her predicament. He ordered her to act like his wife and to feign sleep by resting her head upon his shoulder. The Nazis exchanged salutes with the Fascist officer and permitted his "wife" to continue her nap.

This story conveys the spirit of the Italian people. I am not saying the Italians were all saints. Surely there were among them some quislings, appeasers and squealers. I am, however, saying that the goodness of the Italians was overwhelming.

## LEOPOLD PROCURES A PAROLE

### *Rehabilitation Is Proven Sound*

I started to correspond with Nathan Leopold in 1940 while he was serving a life sentence in Joliet penitentiary in Illinois. You may recall I wrote of my visit to him in 1925, a year after he was sentenced.

His letters were masterpieces, not only in their literary excellence but in the revelation of a man who was rehabilitating himself and by his great work was helping to set precedents for the science of penology.

During World War II Leopold attained great publicity by volunteering as a guinea pig in malaria experiments and persuaded several hundred convicts to permit themselves to be innoculated for making the tests. *Life* magazine had a feature article describing the heroic efforts of Leopold.

There was an appeal made to me to help Leopold get his parole in the early fifties, and naturally I was enthusiastic. His brother Mike whom I had never met, phoned me several times to discuss matters. Among other things, I even offered to employ Leopold.

I contacted a number of clergymen who wrote appeals to Governor Stratton and I wrote the following letter to the governor:

*September 18, 1953*

*Hon. William G. Stratton*
*Governor's Mansion*
*Springfield, Illinois*

*Dear Governor:*

*President Taft had patiently sat through a ninety-minute interview with Rabbi Cohen of Galveston, Texas, and then said;*

*"I sincerely regret my inability to grant the pardon to Mr. X." Then as the President escorted the Rabbi to the door, he continued, "Rabbi, I have great admiration for your people. I marvel that you would come all the way from Galveston to intercede in behalf of a fellow Jew in his unfortunate position."*

*"But, Mr. President," Rabbi Cohen went on to say, "you are mistaken—Mr. X is not a Jew, but is a member of the Greek Orthodox Church." Whereupon the amazed President Taft said, "In that case I must grant a pardon to Mr. X for in truth you have humiliated me by the pure objectivity of your plea and the true nobility of your action."*

*In that spirit, Governor Stratton, I appeal for a pardon for Nathan Leopold.*

*As a classmate of his in 1924, at the University of Chicago Law School, Leopold had nothing but contempt for me. I was as poor as he was rich. I was hard working and industrious as he was an idler and parasite. I was a mediocre, run-of-the-mill kind of student, whereas Leopold was dazzlingly brilliant. While his future seemed assured, the road ahead for me appeared difficult and uncertain.*

*When in May 1924 the world learned about the Loeb-Leopold case, I was among those who longed to see Leo-*

*pold committed to death. His death would have been a triumph for all who envied his apparent good fortune. It was a field day for the haters and unthinking of the world who lusted for the death of these young, cynical and irresponsible murderers.*

*Why do I work and pray for Leopold's pardon today when I wished for him to die in 1924?*

*Simply because the depression, Fascism, Hitlerism, World War II, Korea, the Cold War with Russia, have changed me from a monkey into a man—from an unthinking hater to a thinking person, who will not compromise with love for all mankind—even with mine enemies. That is why I loved the Germans and Japanese people even when we were at war with them. I contributed $2500 to a relocation center for the Japanese of California in 1942—after Pearl Harbor, even though I have never personally met or spoken to a Japanese person in my life.*

*I have become obsessed with the absolute truth taught by our prophets, "Hate the sin but not the sinner."*

*Note the enclosed reprint from Harper's, April 1943. The Jewess, Frau Rathenau, exemplified by her action in the most exalted sense, the wisdom of understanding and forgiving the sinner but hating only evil. Had the state killed the murderer of her son what good would it have done anyone? Instead, her noble and unprecedented action of living rather than giving lip service only to the admonition of Jesus and the prophets of Israel resulted in hundreds of lives being saved. A young murderer turns out to be an extraordinary humanitarian and hero. Why? Only because he was overwhelmed by LOVE and UNDERSTANDING.*

*Can't you see the parallel in the case of Leopold? A young murderer may rot in jail "and waste his spirit in the desert air." On the other hand, if you will ignore the haters and the unthinking—if you will act heroically, as did Frau Rathenau, you will grant a pardon to Nathan Leopold.*

*I will give employment to Leopold. God weaves mysterious designs, and it turned out ironically that I who was despised and loathed by him am eager to help him rehabilitate himself as a man amongst men. He has proven himself to be of great service to penology while paying for the crime of his youth.*

*This appeal, Governor Stratton, does not come from a starry-eyed dreamer, a so-called "do gooder." This appeal is not prompted by anything but the purest and noblest motives. With God's aid I have developed in only fifteen years a business doing over $20,000,000 annually. My contributions to charity are in excess of $1,000,000.*

*Hate and ignorance have been the cause of all the ills of mankind. Hate and ignorance have brought civilization to the precarious position that hydrogen bombs place it in.*

*Before it is too late, it is imperative that all of us cast hate and ignorance out of our being. All of us must become obsessed with the need for exercising love and understanding every day of our lives.*

*You understand then, Governor, that my appeal is prompted only because I try to take seriously "doing justice, loving mercy, and walking humbly with my God."*

*Governor Stratton, it is now your turn to act.*

*From my heart, and with God as a Witness, I am*

*Sincerely yours,*

SAMUEL J. GOLDFARB

When Leopold was paroled he wisely decided to accept the job offer in the Hospital of the Brethren in Puerto Rico. He did wonderful work as an X-ray technician and after two years entered the University of Puerto Rico as a post-graduate student and instructor.

I visited him after his marriage to Trudy Feldman Gomez and enjoyed a lovely luncheon at their modest apartment. Thank God, Nathan Leopold has proven that men can become rehabilitated.

EVELYN VON REIS

## *She Would Rather Be Killed Than Kill*

The Caronia, the most luxurious cruise ship afloat, was our hotel whenever we stopped in any port on our trip to the land of the Midnight Sun.

The wonderful day we spent in Gothenburg, Sweden, we docked early in the morning and sailed about dinner-time. On returning to my stateroom I was surprised to find one of the most beautiful bouquets of flowers I had ever seen. Was the captain of the ship supplying all the passengers with such a treat? There was no anniversary or any other occasion to be celebrated. Who then had sent this exquisite floral piece?

The card I discovered gave me the answer. It said, "I have the feeling I just must send you some flowers." . . . Evelyn Van Reis.

I'd like to tell you about this remarkable lady. Even in all literature I have never read of a noble human being such as she revealed herself to be.

The passengers did the usual things that tourists do with ten or twelve hours in which to see the sights, shop the stores and do whatever pleased them. The number one attraction seemed to be the new, modern Park Hotel. There was a gift shop in the lobby which carried the finest merchandise in the world. Patek-Phillipe watches for one thousand dollars and up were in plentiful supply. Half the passengers on our ship could be seen there. My eyes, however, focused on a single person who fascinated me. I never again expect to see a more beautiful and queenly woman than the one upon whom I was feasting my eyes.

I gathered, from the manner in which she conducted

herself, that she was the proprietor of the establishment. She was not waiting on any customer. I kept staring at her not only because of her beauty, but because to me she appeared as a spiritual vision. More than that I felt compelled to discreetly address her. In a whisper I said, "Madame, I hope that you are not offended by my asking . . . are you a Jewess?" The wonder is that she didn't faint. Her face reflected amazement when she answered, "Yes, I am, but I'm past fifty and no one has ever before asked me that question. Both my father and mother were Jews. I have two brothers who practice medicine in Baltimore and Hartford. Our family name in Amsterdam was Samuels. I am presently married to a Swedish nobleman. Now tell me, who are you?"

That is how it started. For some reason she was interested in the Loeb-Leopold case and felt it an extraordinary coincidence that I was working for Leopold's parole. She was impressed by the fact that despite Leopold's early contempt for me I was, nevertheless, returning good for evil.

Then she said, "You know, Mr. Goldfarb, you are one of the few I have ever known who abhors hate. I love my people, but I have felt that they make fierce haters. Let me tell you of my experience in Auschwitz." She showed me the blue tattooed number on her wrist.

"I was there for almost a year after my parents were killed. I attribute my survival to the fact that all during the nightmare I was determined to my dying gasp not to yield to hatred. I need not tell you it wasn't easy. If I said it once I said it several thousand times, 'It is better to be persecuted than to be a persecutor; it is better to be killed than to be a killer.' Of course, I murmured this to myself no matter how great the horrors I experienced while staring in a glazed look."

The end of our discussion found us both obsessed with

the need for hate eradication to give hope for a better world. I, however, felt humble. Here I was face to face with one who was put to a test as great as any in the history of human suffering. She came through. I could only say the words . . . preach our common exalted obsession.

I pray to God that Evelyn Von Reis is alive and in good health. I hope she learns, perhaps through her brothers, that the story of her heroism and idealism which vies with that of Job and Jesus, has at least been recorded for the world to know.

RETURNING GOOD FOR EVIL

## *I Establish the Good Heart Award*

During his first year at the University of Miami in 1957, our youngest son, Alan, did not do well scholastically, but even worse he had no social life.

We thought that joining a fraternity, Phi Sigma Delta, would benefit him. Instead, the boys took advantage of Alan's timidity and shyness and never gave him the feeling of belonging.

At the annual affair at the plush Fontainbleau Hotel the boys played a series of practical jokes, funny to them, but humiliating to Alan. The faculty adviser, Mr. John Wilcox, informed me that Alan was treated outrageously.

The following afternoon after Alan was exposed to a nightmarish ordeal we met him for early Sunday dinner to comfort him. My instinctive feeling was to dynamite the fraternity house but sober second judgment dictated that I do something constructive.

I was inspired with an idea which I felt would procure

decent treatment for Alan and at the same time elevate the values and behavior of the group. I phoned Mr. Wilcox and got his wholehearted approval.

This was the result. I was invited to be the guest speaker at the "open house" evening on January 14, 1958. When called upon to speak I delivered the following talk:

*Gentlemen of Phi Sigma Delta:*

*Ever since my son was pledged to your house it has been my hope to do something of lasting value for your fraternity.*

*This feeling was aroused when a rival group rushing Alan said to me, "Mr. Goldfarb, Phi Sigma Delta is rated lowest on the campus." My answer was that I would prefer any group to one so unkind as to rate human beings.*

*Subsequently in visiting here I observed many houses larger and more impressive than yours. I could understand how unthinking, immature youth might look down their noses at a fraternity which couldn't boast the best athletes, scholars, musicians or what have you. Perhaps it is true that Phi Sigma Delta isn't noted for anything extraordinary.*

*Now I have an idea which might bring honor, glory and recognition to your fraternity.*

*Phi Sigma Delta could be the first fraternity on the campus where each year a deserving brother is selected to receive—*

THE GOOD HEART AWARD

*The individual so honored would have his name engraved on an appropriate beautiful silver loving cup and in addition would receive a handsome cash prize.*

*Now let me tell you a bit about the thinking that entered into this idea.*

*First, I was reminded of the famous discussion held by great scholars as to which is the most important organ of the body.*

*The eyes, ears, nose, arms, etc., etc., each had someone to argue in its behalf.*

*The scholar who argued in behalf of the heart easily won when he proved that one can live briefly without any organ of the body but not without a heart.*

*Remember then that overwhelmingly the heart is man's most important possession.*

*Consider Hitler and the men surrounding him. Among them were the greatest in business, finance, athletics, education. They had brains enough to almost conquer the world.*

*Hitler and his cohorts had everything but good hearts.*

*In contrast consider how fortunate we have been in our leadership. From Washington, Adams and Jefferson thru both Roosevelts, Wilson, Truman, and Eisenhower. They were human and had faults but all were men with good hearts.*

*Why is Abraham Lincoln revered throughout the world? He was homely, gawky, a failure in business. He couldn't dance and was a flop socially.*

*Lincoln is revered because he had compassion and understanding that emanates from a good heart.*

*Now how about you? Have you got good hearts? If not why not? You may become successful lawyers, doctors, engineers, businessmen. Remember you may still be failures as human beings if you fail to appreciate that a good heart is more important than any other asset in life.*

*The prophet Micah asked, "What doth the Lord require of thee but that thou do justice—love mercy and walk humbly with thy God?"*

*That requires a good heart!*

*Wouldn't it be wonderful if in time Phi Sigma Delta became noted for being the fraternity with a heart? Could you aspire to greater distinction?*

*I look back on my own youth. I remember little kindness, fair play or consideration. I was cross eyed until I was 16 and a midget until 18. I was the only boy on the campus of Washington University wearing knee length pants.*

*I was never permitted to enter games. They called me cockeye, runt and humiliating names.*

*I was too poor and too ignorant to be asked to join a fraternity. I attended no affairs. . . . I had no social life.*

*I bear no ill will toward those who made life a hell on earth for me in those days. It is with genuine sorrow that I have observed so many of them, especially the more thoughtless ones—turn out to be failures.*

*One of my classmates at the law school committed the most notorious crime of this century. Nathan Leopold was 19 years old when with Richard Loeb he murdered Bobby Franks.*

*Perhaps you have read the book or seen the play in New York titled "Compulsion." It tells all about the famous Loeb-Leopold Case.*

*Leopold ignored me because I was a nobody. I was as poor as he was rich. I was as mediocre as he was brilliant. I was as naive as he was sophisticated.*

*Leopold talked down to me as if I were a monkey instead of a person. He did everything to make me feel as if I did not belong to the human race.*

*Am I glad that he has been imprisoned for the past 33 years? Do I hate his guts?*

*On the contrary I have nothing but compassion and understanding for him.*

*The fact is I have been corresponding with him for many years.*

*Furthermore I have tried for the past 4 years to get him paroled. I have here with me, for any of you who care to see it, a letter received from Leopold's lawyer last week—now hold on to your seats—listen to this—if Leopold is freed next month—he is going to work for one of the Goldfarb Enterprises.*

*Leopold can read and write 27 languages. Leopold as my class mate had everything. Not one but two automobiles of his own—*

*He had wine—women—song*

*Tragically the one thing HE DID NOT HAVE was a good heart.*

*To-day he is O.K. Someday I will be pleased to tell you why this is true.*

*So getting back to those thoughtless young fellows who said Phi Sigma Delta was rated the lowest—for them too I have only compassion and understanding.*

*May it come to pass that with God's aid you gentlemen have the courage, wisdom and inspiration to make your fraternity stand for something—something good—Yea—even something great.*

*Gentlemen of Phi Sigma Delta! If you are interested I stand here ready to help establish at your fraternity an annual award to be a blessing to this house—*

*THE GOOD HEART AWARD!*

The boys and their guests for the evening were most enthusiastic about accepting my offer.

A few weeks later we held ceremonies to dedicate The Good Heart Award. Present were officials of the University, the entire membership of the fraternity and many important guests.

Over the fireplace in the large living room there had been erected a magnificent bronze installation, beautifully designed and artistically engraved to explain the meaning and purpose of the Award. It was altogether a dignified and inspiring affair.

For the remaining months that Alan stayed at the University he was treated with respect and affection by everyone. The boys apparently appreciated the fact that no further reference was ever made to the treatment Alan had received.

I have always known that constructive effort serves

to inspire youth. In this case we knew that it paid to return good for evil.

PHILANTHROPY

## *A Palliative But Not a Cure*

Many people are mistaken in their judgment of the rich when they learn about a big gift made by a wealthy person to a charitable cause.

Tax advantages often accrue to the wealthy that do not exist for those of modest income. When the rich man gives fifty thousand dollars to the March of Dimes the probability is that not much of it comes out of his own pocket. Probably ninety per cent is tax deductible, so that in effect, he is giving mostly Uncle Sam's money. In any case the tycoon is making no great sacrifice and depriving himself of little. The steel worker or any other laborer that gives five dollars to the March of Dimes is taking it out of his pocket and is denying his family or himself the benefit of what five dollars could purchase.

Would it surprise you to learn that I, who have been consecrated to philanthropy, hope that some day it will not exist? When that day comes the world will be so ordered that no person will require assistance from another person. There will be no poverty. All people will buy insurance in a cooperative, mutual trust similar to Blue Cross so that when they require aid from a powerful institution they will go to the one they themselves have helped to create and support.

Visualize a housewife sweeping up the dirt on the floor. Instead of putting it in the dust pan she sweeps it under the sofa. One can't see the dirt, but it exists and is in the house. To my way of thinking, those who are committed to the doctrine of philanthropy are like that indifferent housewife. They are only ameliorating a situation, but they have done nothing to eliminate the necessity for a person to humiliate himself by seeking help from another.

It is true that until that time arrives when there is no need for philanthropy we should all support it. Our eyes, however, should be looking ahead to the future. In that case, concurrently with our present philanthropy, we should be working even harder to create a society where no one need come to another for assistance.

Happily we are on the right road today. Since the great depression our government has realized that it has the important function of planning for the good and welfare of all its citizens. It protects the peoples' savings. It provides a system for social security. It enacts wage and hour laws to create a higher standard of living. It has brought about social security and is now trying to create medicare and all other benefits to take care of its citizens from the cradle to the grave.

The growth of labor unions has helped the prosperity of the country and increasingly brought to those who produce by their sweat a greater percentage of the value of their production.

Abraham Lincoln, great prophet that he was, had the vision to see it as far back as December 3, 1861 when in his first annual message to Congress he said, "Inasmuch as most good things are produced by labor, it follows that all such things ought to belong to those whose labor has produced them. But it has happened in all ages of the world that some have labored, and others without labor, have enjoyed a larger proportion of the fruits. This is wrong and should not continue. To secure to each laborer the whole product of his labor as nearly as possible is a worthy object of any good government."

I sent this passage from Lincoln's text to Henry Wallace, then secretary of Commerce, and Walter Reuther, head of the C.I.O. labor organization. Both were grateful to me for bringing it to their attention and the latter wrote to me enthusiastically on November 7, 1945 that it came in the nick of time as he was having it incorporated in the brief that was then being prepared for their negotiations with General Motors.

Many of our large corporations are helping to bring about the day when private philanthropy will be made unnecessary. They are setting up bonus plans such as Lincoln Electric in Cleveland and profit sharing plans as great Sears Roebuck has had for years.

Great government, cooperating with powerful labor and enlightened business management will in time cure the economic evils in our society. Then philanthropy will not be necessary. We will have a society that precludes the need for it.

Isn't it better to obtain a cure rather than to go along forever using a palliative?

## THE ALL IMPORTANT QUESTION

## *Am I a Jew . . . or An American?*

I am both! To ask one which he loves more, his Jewishness or Americanism, is like asking, "Whom do you love better, your wife or your mother?"

Does one love his wife less because he loves his mother? The Talmud says that no matter how devoted a son is to his mother he must favor his wife when a choice becomes imperative. So in a showdown I would favor America.

I do not, however, go along with Stephen Decatur who

said, "My country, may she always be right, but right or wrong, my country." I prefer saying that I hope my country is always right, but if she be wrong, God help me and others to make her right. If we fail then I would take refuge in God.

To me loyalty to God takes priority over loyalty to country. I reason this way:

*The whole is greater than any of its parts. God is the whole! All else is only a part, not excluding the great and mighty U.S.A. In any crisis I will cling to God rather than to any part of God.*

It depresses me to hear of those who shout, "America First" and wave our flag the most. Too often I find such people to be immature. They are creatures of emotion rather than reason. They consider it divided loyalty for Jews to love the State of Israel.

My answer to them is, "Beware of the man who disowns his mother when he takes on a wife."

The great Supreme Court Justice Brandeis answered such an attack by saying, "If I am a good Jew that is a guarantee of my being a good American."

I appeal to my fellow Jews not to be intimidated or misled by flag-wavers and epithet-hurlers. Let your mind and conscience be your guide. The Jew that is fully developed spiritually will take pride in his Jewishness as well as his Americanism.

DOCTOR ARTHUR COMPTON

## *Considered Greatest American*

It was a delightful luncheon at the very edge of the ocean front of the hotel which advertises itself as being the most luxurious in all the world.

My host was Leon Lowenstein, head of the firm bearing his name. Charlie Richter, a vice-president of the Corn Chemical Bank of New York, was the other member of our trio.

Suddenly Joe Di Maggio, the baseball great, came into the outdoor dining area. He was followed by an entourage of gorgeous girls and several gentlemen.

This prompted Mr. Richter to remark that in our country adulation was given to celebrities in the world of sport and entertainment rather than to those who achieve greatness in intellectual pursuits.

As if God wanted to prove this observation I turned my head and spotted someone whom I believed to be the very man Pearl Buck, in a recent *Reader's Digest* article, referred to as the greatest living American.

I asked my two friends to excuse me and sauntered over to the table where Mr. Great was lunching with a lady.

Addressing him I said, "Pardon sir, you are Dr. Compton?" He answered, "Yes, and this is Mrs. Compton," as he referred to the lady. He asked whether I would care to join them. I told him I had just finished lunch but would be pleased to sit with them. I told them my name and said I recognized him only from pictures I had seen in periodicals.

Jocularly he remarked, "Recognizing me will cost me

an orange. I bet Mrs. Compton that in my four day stay in Miami Beach no one would know who I was."

Dr. Compton and his brother were notables at the Massachusetts Institute of Technology. Each had won the Nobel Prize independently. The reason Pearl Buck gave for considering him so outstanding was the fact that President Truman would not make use of the atom bomb unless he first gave his approval.

I told Dr. Compton that I had attended Washington University many years before he had become Chancellor of that fine school. "In that case I hope you do not mind my considering you one of my boys and asking you to tell me of some of your accomplishments," he said.

I answered without delay, "Producing more women's and children's dresses than anyone in America is an accomplishment, but aptly described by the preacher in Ecclesiastes when he said, "Vanity, vanity, all is vanity." Being described by Dorothy Thompson as the first fanatical democrat she had ever met was satisfying as was Henry Montor's reference to me on my fiftieth birthday when he wrote, 'You, more than any other man in America, established the principle that we owe a tithe of our possessions to our brothers.' I was proud to have established the Good Heart Award in the school systems of Paris, Rome, Athens and especially in Linz, Austria where Hitler and Eichman had been reared. Also, I was pleased to have created the slogan to 'Do Business on Monday in the Spirit of Sunday.' "

Dr. Compton's face lit up and with a broad smile said, "Goldfarb, you will be interested to hear about the time I entertained Dr. Romulo when he was president of the Philippines. I asked him what special favor I might do for him and he said he was most anxious to pay a visit to a Quaker Church. I took Dr. Romulo to a Quaker meeting house near Philadelphia. We entered and quietly seated ourselves. We remained absolutely silent for about twenty-five minutes when an elderly lady arose and said, 'Unless someone wishes to offer testimony I suggest that our meeting be ended.' A moment of silence ensued, then everyone arose and walked out of the hall.

"A bewildered look appeared on Dr. Romulo's face as we met a Quaker friend outdoors. 'Tell me,' uttered the great gentleman from the Philippines, 'why is it I saw no dais, no pulpit, no preacher nor did I hear any sermon nor hymns or any prayers. All was silent—when did the services begin?' My friend then answered President Romulo, 'Your Excellency, with the Quakers service begins when members leave the church.' "

That story was Dr. Compton's way of showing approval of my slogan to "Do Business on Monday in the Spirit of Sunday."

Returning to Mr. Lowenstein and Mr. Richter's table they were astounded to learn that so noted a gentleman was not recognized by them. One mentioned, however, that he had read in the morning paper that Dr. Compton was to participate as head of the Protestants in America in the National Conference of Christians and Jews.

As we three arose to walk back to the cabana we passed the gay, crowded tables of the Di Maggio followers. It was plain to see that in our society the multitude reserved their adulation for those who were prominent either in athletics or show business.

AUSTRIA

## *Great Music, Fine Steel, Good Hearts*

In Vienna in 1951 I was eager to see the spot where the Jews in silk hats and frock coats were made to scrub the streets during Hitler's time. Luck favored me. I saw a candy shop on the Graben called Altman and Kuehne. Entering it I asked whether the Fifth Avenue shop by the same name in New York had any connection. The attractive lady manager told me of Mr. Altman's leaving for New York just prior to Hitler taking over Austria and that she had been in his employ for many years.

She took me to the corner where "the most tragic picture I ever saw" was taken. She told me she had witnessed that scene and many others and was convinced that the individual Austrian proved to be more cruel than the individual German. As a matter of fact she moved to Berlin for several years prior to Hitler's downfall and observed that the Berliners behaved in a more civilized fashion and were less barbaric than the Austrians.

Eight years later in 1959 I spent a week at Bad Gastein in Austria. From there we took a train to Linz, Austria to see an eye specialist for my wife. We were in a compartment on the train with a lady and her eighteen-year-old son. He spoke English sufficiently for us to communicate. I asked him for what Austria was noted and, like a reflex action, the answer was on the tip of his tongue. "Austria," he said, "was noted for three things . . . great music, fine steel and good hearts."

At the mention of good hearts, it recalled my visit with the candy store manager in Vienna and the Good Heart Award set up at the University of Miami in 1958.

Then followed a discussion in which I pointed out to

him that the Austrians practiced brutality and savagery even more than the Germans. Coincidentally, the two most sinister figures in modern times were named Adolf and both spent their entire school lives in Linz, Austria where I was headed. (By the way will anyone ever again name a baby "Adolf"?)

Having pointed out to this young fellow the irony of claiming good heartedness as a special Austrian quality, as if he were referring to strudel, I went on to explain that not only had I no hatred for Austrians, but not even for the two monsters named Adolf.

This boy knowing I was a Jew and still expressing myself as I did, was visibly moved. He told me of his plan to become a concert pianist. As I got off at Linz he kissed my hand and told me he would always remember the thoughts I had conveyed to him.

After seeing the doctor, our chauffeur stopped at a graveyard to point to a grave where Herr Schickelgruber —Hitler's father was buried. At mid-afternoon my wife went to town to do some shopping and I stayed at the hotel lost in thoughts. In my mind I saw again the picture of those Jews with silk hats and frock coats scrubbing the street while their Nazi tormentors were laughing in hyena fashion. I remembered the words of the candy store manager. I recalled reading *Mein Kampf*. I remembered reading of Eichman's blind, ruthless efficiency in being chief slaughterer of six million Jews. And I remembered only an hour ago hearing a delicate, innocent Austrian piano player refer to the good hearts of the Austrians. I am one who believes that the same brutal savages in Austria during the 1938 through 1944 period could prove to be as gentle as lambs if their leader were a Franz Joseph instead of an Adolf Hitler. I am one who believes that if a "Hitler" seized power in the United States the majority of Americans would turn into destructive animals. Yes, IT CAN HAPPEN HERE as long as people mumble pious words in their church on Sunday and behave as bigots on Monday.

This kind of thinking inspired me with an idea. Why not set up a Good Heart Award such as I did at the University of Miami, in the very city where Hitler and Eichman attended twelve years of schooling? Give the people of Linz a chance to show their contempt for hate and cruelty.

With this in mind I called the English speaking manager and invited him to have a drink in my room where I told him of my idea. I said I would like for him to arrange a meeting with the powers that be in the community to present my idea of the Good heart Award in the Linz high schools.

The manager arranged for me to meet with the president of the Board of Education and his associates at a breakfast meeting the following morning. The gentlemen were set on fire by my idea. They told me that Linz was the only city in Europe where the *Diary of Anne Frank* could not be shown because lingering Nazism gripped enough hooligans to stir up trouble. They regretted that the absence of the Burgomaster (Mayor) of the city precluded giving me an official answer. I told them I would be at the Imperial Hotel in Vienna for a week.

On Tuesday I received a long distance call early in the morning from the president of the Board of Education. They would arrive at my hotel about eleven A.M. and asked that I have an interpreter present. Punctually the group from Linz entered the hotel lobby. With the group were reporters for the Associated Press and Reuters.

The committee from Linz brought a contract with them which in German is called Stifftung. This contract was for one hundred years between the Province of Linz, Austria and the Samuel J. Goldfarb Foundation. The school system of Linz agreed to select each year from the graduating class of all the high schools one person to whom would be given the Good Heart Award.

My charity and educational fund guaranteed to present each year the one hundred dollar cash award and the hand-engraved scroll to the winner.

When the interpreters made all points clear to all concerned, the Stifftung was signed and copies handed over to me and retained by the members of the Board of Education. I then invited the entire group to be my luncheon guests in that luxurious dining room at the Imperial. During the course of the luncheon the gentlemen from Linz were bubbling over with good spirits and expressed their appreciation for an action which they felt would always be spiritually uplifting to their community and to all of Austria.

One of the men then asked in what other cities had I planned to establish the award. I told him that I had had no idea of setting up the award elsewhere but since he mentioned it I would try. Happily my endeavors succeeded for in subsequent weeks I established the Good Heart Award in the public school systems of Rome, Paris, Athens, and Istanbul.

With God's aid I hope to establish the award in a key city in every country of the world. I hope that in doing so I am planting a seed which will inspire the masses to put their faith in men rather than in monkeys. It is so easy to identify the monkey who seeks to become a leader. The Greeks said, "By their gifts ye shall know them." I say, "By their hearts ye shall know them." If a man expresses negative thoughts about any human beings he must be branded as a monkey. If he expresses himself only positively as have all our American presidents, then he reveals himself to be a man.

May it be the will of God that monkeys never again become leaders of the people.

## *Cancer of the Soul*

On the night of January 18, 1960 a gala affair was given in honor of Jennie Grossinger and me at the Hollywood Beach Hotel in Hollywood, Florida. It was sponsored by the Jewish Theological Seminary and we were given their Eternal Light Award.

To me it appeared as a gathering for the most affluent Jews in Florida. Our host, Ben Tobin, owner of the hotel, was seated next to me. In chatting we discovered that we were both born near each other in the same province in Russia.

When called upon I delivered this talk:

*"Dr. Finkelstein, Dr. Arzt, my dear friend Jennie, Chairmen of this magnificent dinner, and all who grace this room with their presence:*

*I feel deeply moved by the honor bestowed upon me and interpret it to mean that I must set my sights higher and do all possible to reach out to God. . . .*

*I have come here tonight to receive, and want to reciprocate by giving. For years I have been concerned about a matter that threatens the downfall of civilization. I believe we have more to fear from this behavior phenomenon on the part of people in our society than we do from possible attack by the hydrogen bomb.*

*I want to give to you the benefit of my thinking. I talk to you about a disease more devastating than cancer. Cancer destroys the body, whereas this disease destroys the soul. I call it Money-itis. It is the condition where one loves money more than God.*

*We have lived with cancer and other diseases for centuries. We can go on living with them ad-infinitum. If, however, money-itis becomes more widespread, we will follow the pattern of the mighty Roman Empire which disintegrated and crumbled. Even as Nero fiddled while Rome burned, so do those with money-itis go about accumulating . . . getting . . . forever preoccupied with money and power and giving a mere "handout" to institutions that cry out for support.*

*Only a few weeks ago, I read in important magazines about two families, each of whom started with little, less than fifteen years ago, and are now each worth in excess of $50,000,000. It will be interesting to observe what they will do with the tens of millions in excess of their need for security and pleasure. I wrote to each of these families and told them that if they love God more than money, then in that case their giving will keep pace with their getting.*

*In this connection let me point out to you that children whose forebearers set up charitable foundations have for the most part turned out to be men and women respected by the community. On the other hand, take note of the extremely wealthy who are notorious for their scandalous behaviour. Rarely will you find their super-wealthy parents were noted for being charitable. In the case of money-itis it is passed on to the children at least 99 out of 100 times. Here it is truly the case of "Monkey sees—monkey does." If Papa or Mama loves money and hates to give, why should the child and grandchild do otherwise?*

*If money-itis becomes more prevalent, it means that the institutions serving God can't do their jobs. In that case child delinquency flourishes, mental disturbance rages like a forest fire and it's only a matter of time when our civilization, as we know it, will go the way of all* pleasure-mad *materialistic nations. In plain words, we may go to HELL!*

*We must never forget our humble beginnings. Where did we or our fathers begin on our road to financial affluence? What did we have to start with and what have we accumulated? If perchance our giving has not kept pace with our getting, how about making a contribution to the Seminary to set matters right? Personally, on this night, I want to announce that I am bringing up my previous gift to the Seminary to total $60,000.*

*God bless all of you and may it be His Will that none of our children or grandchildren ever be affected with money-itis!"*

It didn't occur to me that there were so many rabbis in the audience until they lined up in front of the dais to congratulate me and many asked for permission to deliver sermons based on *Money-itis*. At least to clergymen it was not far-fetched to say it was cancer of the soul.

Nothing disturbs me more than to witness people living like lords . . . magnificent home, two Cadillacs in the carport and all that goes with it, but who fail to give $100 a year to the needy.

My concern is particularly great for Jews who fail to give to the United Jewish Appeal. They lived during Hitlerism and were aware of the greatest atrocities since creation and still did nothing to aid the unfortunates.

In 1940 at a United Jewish Appeal breakfast in Woodmere, Long Island, I met professor Chamberlin of Columbia University. He contributed $1,000 annually to United Jewish Appeal insisting that Gentiles too had an obligation to support this cause. That is why in April 1964 at a United Jewish Appeal dinner in Sarasota I said, "Jews who fail to contribute to United Jewish Appeal are spiritually delinquent.

A friend of mine drew $100,000 annual salary and reported $800,000 profit during the year. The revenue department allowed him to give $20,000 from his salary and $40,000 from his profits to charity. Under pressure he yielded to the extent of giving me a $2,000 pledge with these words, "Sam, I can't figure out men like you . . . there is a pig inside of me and it hurts me to give." Not too long after that he died leaving over $1,000,000 insurance besides his fortune in business and investments. Shortly after that his lovely wife remarried a fine gentleman and life marches on while my friend lies in the cold grave. He had money-itis. He never lived. He merely existed. For to live is to give . . . never forget that. In the last decade of his life he could have given $50,000 a year to charity . . . for a total of $500,000. Instead of leaving a fortune totalling $6,000,000 he would have left $5,900,000 (of the $500,000 he could have given to charity Uncle Sam would have paid $400,000 and he only $100,000.) I ask you wasn't he a fool?

There are too, too many foolish people who fail to figure it out. Too many who love money more than God. Too many with cancer of the soul.

Do you recognize the type who for himself must have everything of the best . . . and everything first? Color television is developed and he rushes to be first to have it. He buys the newest and most costly automobiles and the largest and most expensive houses in town and country. He buys loads of jewelry and expensive paintings. Check his record as to thinking about the less fortunate and you'll be shocked to see what a midget he has become.

I know a man whose wife's jewels are appraised at close to a million dollars, he plays gin rummy at a dollar a point; I witnessed his placing a $25,000 bet on a horse to win. I could never get him to give $1,000 to United Jewish Appeal. True, that is an exceptional case, but in lesser degree you will find tens of thousands who fail to give 1% of what it costs them to live. Is there any excuse for anyone spending $20,000 a year to live and not give $200 a year to charity?

What happens to the children who are reared in homes where Papa and Mama think only of themselves and find nothing too good or expensive, but avoid going to a charity affair as if it were a plague? What example do parents with money-itis set for their children?

Not alone for God's sake, but more particularly for their own sakes do I appeal to the non-givers of America to cut out the cancer, the spiritual blindness that makes life for them a mere existence. Let them desert the ranks of those with money-itis and join those who by good giving know what it is to enjoy good living.

## DIVORCE AFTER 36 YEARS OF MARRIAGE

### *It's Never Too Late to Correct a Mistake*

Mrs. Smith of Maine has tossed her bonnet in the ring and seeks the Republican nomination for president of the United States.

Fantastic! It seems only yesterday that women were given the right to vote. Only 40 years ago most people were super-critical of women who bobbed their hair. As a little boy of six I would peek through the heavily-curtained window of a restaurant to see those "horrible" women who dared to smoke cigarettes.

Women have come a long way from 1920 when they became "emancipated." On the over-all picture I believe they have become superior to their grandmothers in body and mind. In one area they have failed. Many are becoming increasingly inferior as wives. That is the greatest reason why the divorce rate is climbing. Men, on the other hand, have in this past half century become more solicitous and better understanding of their wives. There are many exceptions. It is not a black and white picture. There are plenty of poor husbands and wonderful wives. However, when a count is taken it is probable that there are more good husbands than wives.

Prior to their "emancipation," women were "slaves" to the kitchen, to their children and too often to their husbands. The male spouse of old was in the nature of an autocrat. I remember when my father took his afternoon nap that we were policed by our mother and we dared not raise our voices to disturb him. Today Papa is lucky indeed if the children afford him such luxury.

I have read many stories dealing with unhappy marriages. "Adversary in His Own House" by Stone tells of the opposition Eugene Debs encountered from his wife. Many have said this man, who several times was Socialist candidate for president, was a modern-day saint. Tolstoy, the great Russian novelist, was past eighty when he could no longer endure his miserable marriage. He walked out of his home into a blizzard with the temperature way below zero. Dale Carnegie, in his "Lincoln the Unknown," deals exclusively with the Great Emancipator's unhappy marriage. The last paragraph on page eighty-six reads as follows: "Once, Mrs. Lincoln attacked her husband so savagely and kept it up so long, that even he . . . 'with malice toward none; with charity for all' . . . even he lost his self-control and seizing her by the arm he forced her across the kitchen and pushed her toward the door, saying: 'You're ruining my life. You're making a hell of this house. Now, damn you, you get out of it.' "

It would have been unfair for these men to be criticized if they had sought divorce to obtain peace. In any case no person should pass judgment on another until they have heard both sides of the story.

I was divorced after being married thirty-six years. On October 15, 1962 I married Celia Friedman, a lovely 57-year-old widow. Since that day I have known peace of mind.

After honeymooning in California, I took Celia to St. Louis and New Orleans to meet my family. They too fell in love with her. They were thrilled at seeing I had now found happiness in marriage.

Celebrating our first anniversary I realized that the most wonderful thing that ever happened to me was my marriage to Celia. I now live blissfully with a wife whom I love, respect and admire. She is my companion, sweetheart and friend. Our home is not just a beautiful house but a place of harmony, laughter and contentment. My blood pressure, which had been skyhigh for many years, is now normal.

Is it any wonder that I would like to shout it from the housetops for all the world to hear, "It is never too late to correct a mistake."

## WHOSE PICTURE IS THAT?

## *The Story About One Man in a Million*

In our lovely home in Sarasota a picture hangs on the living room wall. Hundreds of guests have seen this picture and always it prompts one seeing it for the first time to ask, "Whose picture is that?" I then explain to the one inquiring the fascinating story of the subject of the picture and how it came into my possession.

One day I was inspired to write a short essay titled "Whose Picture is That?" so that when the question is put to me I simply supply the person with the written answer. This has proved to be practical as the question is usually asked when the visitor is about to leave.

ONE MAN IN A MILLION

I believe the reader will also enjoy learning the answer to "Whose Picture is That?" and the written explanation is therefore included in my collection of vignettes:

It is not a painting by a famous artist. It is merely a photograph of a kindly but strong looking gentleman. He is revealed from the chest up to his neatly groomed hair. His monarchial uniform is bedecked with many medals. He is King Christian X of Denmark, who reigned from 1912–1947.

The picture, only fifteen inches in length and twelve inches wide, is in a classic gilt wooden frame with a delicately carved crown on its top.

I believe the story associated with my procuring that picture is an interesting one and I am going to tell you about it.

*In 1953 I was in Copenhagen shopping in the fabric department of one of the large stores.*

*I found many exciting new prints and engaged several clerks in cutting off narrow swatches. They were obviously bewildered by my need for countless designs. I could not get them to understand that as a large producer of women's and children's fashions, these patterns were valuable to me.*

*Apparently a clerk telephoned some higher authority and suddenly I was confronted by a fine looking man. He spoke English well and introduced himself as the president of the establishment.*

*He explained that the clerks waiting on me, as well as those from other departments, were flabbergasted by my enormous appetite for swatches of their prints. I explained to him my desire to use them for fashions in America. He was pleased and invited me to come upstairs to visit in his office.*

*We spoke about the University of California, which his daughter was then attending. We discussed supermar-*

*kets, discount stores and other topics of interest to merchants and manufacturers.*

*I was struck by the photograph hanging behind his back. I said, "I must get a picture of King Christian X before leaving Denmark."*

*The merchant was curious to know why I was so eager to have a picture of the King.*

*I told him that I am Jewish and felt certain that for eternity, Jews would remember the bravery and nobility exhibited by his King when the Nazis invaded Denmark. In the dark days of Hitlerism the Jews were ordered to wear yellow arm bands on their sleeves.*

*It was then that King Christian X amazed the peoples of the entire world when he put a yellow arm band around his coat sleeve. Then he mounted his magnificent white horse and rode through the streets of the capital in full defiance of Hitler's order.*

*The department store owner was obviously moved by my explanation. He pleaded with me to have the privilege of sending his secretary out on the town to locate a good photograph of the King. He said, "Your time is limited for the remainder of your stay in Denmark. I will procure and deliver it to your hotel."*

*I was then escorted by him to the elevator and went downstairs to pick up the packages of fabric swatches I had selected.*

*I was disappointed and puzzled when I found the packages were not ready. It appeared to me as if the clerks were deliberately stalling for time. In a few minutes my surmise was corroborated. Again I saw the smiling face of the store owner approaching me. This time, however, he was holding the beautifully framed photograph that we had talked about in his office.*

*Pointing to the picture, he said, "You Americans believe you can do everything better and faster than others. Well, here is one time we prove it isn't always true. In the few minutes since you left my office we not only procured a photograph of King Christian, but already we had it framed and here I am to deliver it."*

*Now it was my turn to be touched—to the point of keeping back the tears. "No, I cannot take this picture from you. I won't have it."*

*The generous Dane made me yield and accept when he told me, "Sir, this picture has been in my office for years and never has anyone commented about it. It occurred to me that in your home or office this picture—the very one that caught your attention, would better serve the memory of our King."*

Indeed, he was right. Many times—too numerous for me to remember, I have had to explain to visitors the story about King Christian X. I have made his courage and nobility known to hundreds simply because they saw his photograph in our home.

RICHES MAKE MEN "SONS O' BITCHES"

## That's Why the World Is in a Mess

At a time in my career when my business was netting around one million dollars a year profit I had contempt for most men of wealth and affluence. I never remember being more excited about reading a single paragraph than when I read the following in 1949:

*"I am more than a little puzzled to account for the instances I have seen of business success. . . . money getting. It comes from a rather low instinct. Certainly it is scarcely met with in a combination with the finer or more interesting traits of character. I have known a great many 'successful' men and a less interesting crowd I do not care to encounter. Not one I have ever known would*

*I care to meet again in this world or the next. A set of mere money getters . . . they were essentially unattractive."*

Where do you suppose I read this? In some Communist magazine? No . . . it was the November issue of *Fortune,* the magazine dedicated to business. Who was the author? A radical, socialist or other brand of left-winger? No! It was Charles Francis Adams, the only man who could claim two grandparents as presidents of the United States, John Adams and John Quincy Adams. In 1905 he made this statement when he was Ambassador of the United States to Czarist Russia.

Recently a columnist in the *Miami Herald* writing about that period says, "Robber barons of finance made millions in railroads, oil, steel and there were no laws to curb their rapacious grabbing. There never was a time when dishonesty in public office was more rampant." Years earlier, the fabulous Commodore Vanderbilt openly sneered, "Let the public be damned."

It was the time when many lives were lost in labor strife at Colorado Fuel and Iron, then owned by the senior John D. Rockefeller. In Pullman, Indiana the casualties were high and blood was being spilled because the rich were too damn selfish and stingy to pay the workmen a living wage.

Did you ever see the mansions in Newport and the breathtaking establishments on Fifth Avenue that were built at that time? Did you ever see Charley Schwab's palatial block square palace on Riverside Drive, built early in the century?

Never did so few do so much for themselves and so little for those struggling to earn five hundred dollars a year as did those contemptible, blood-sucking capitalists in that Crinoline Age.

It's enough to make one's blood curdle and one's hair to

shoot straight up in the air to read of the extravagant parties costing tens of thousands of dollars.

Nero was a piker! He only fiddled while Rome burned. It is my contention that the rich and affluent at the turn of the century could have prevented both World Wars and all war from ever happening again.

I charge the greedy capitalists with such lack of vision as to result in over one hundred million lives being unnecessarily lost from the turn of the century to the present time.

Did it occur to these callous, selfish and ruthless robber barons that they had it in their power to present, free of charge, the equivalent of today's air-conditioned bungalow to every family in the world, even in darkest Africa? The price? Far less than the cost of the wars that have occurred since 1900.

Who could have done it? How could they do it? The one thousand richest and most affluent families in the world could have prevented war from ever happening again. How? By holding a meeting in which they dedicated their thoughts, their fortunes and their lives to the abolition of poverty and prejudice, and creating a world of peace and plenty.

Think of it! One family, the Rothschilds, had it in their power to create or destroy any number of individual empires. Can you imagine the force for good that would have come about if this one family joined forces with the Vanderbilts, Carnegies, Rockefellers, Thyssens, Krupps, Sassoons and the remaining nine hundred and ninety-three families that held the economy of the world in the palms of their hands?

Only the sky would have limited the programs for the good and welfare of mankind that would have resulted from such vision.

To be sure, among one thousand there was a handful

of decent families, notably the Rothschilds, Carnegies and a repentant John D. Rockefeller, Sr. Today it is a different story. There are many enlightened rich men and their number is increasing. The fact that a backward country like Russia surpassed us in developing nuclear weapons opened the eyes and minds of all Americans.

Unfortunately there are still too many men of wealth to whom Mr. Adams' criticism still applies. I pray for the time when the top ten thousand families on the "success ladder" pool their interests and their thoughts and consecrate themselves to bringing about a world where poverty and prejudice exist no more.

Then philanthropy will be as unnecessary as an appendix is to the human body. Then I am sure Mr. Charles Francis Adams will be at St. Peter's side as these men of wealth are welcomed inside the pearly gates.

A HORRIBLE WORLD?

## *We Can Be the World We Want*

One morning in 1947 my son Gene entered my office excitedly to tell me that walking down Central Park West he glanced at the bulletin in front of a church and read that the sermon to be preached on Sunday was titled, "We Must Be the World We Want."

I told my son it was one of the finest expressions I had ever heard in my life and that it behooved us to make that statement an integral part of our lives.

A number of times thereafter my sons and I discussed the phrase. It occurred to us that whatever we found unpleasant in the world need not exist in our lives if we create the "world we want."

What kind of world do we want? A world at peace? A

world wherein love annihilates hate, where hope displaces despair, where courage deposes fear? Do we want a world where truth, sincerity, compassion and understanding prevail?

Then all we have to do is rid ourselves of all negative thoughts and actions. We should think and act peaceably, love our neighbors, have faith and act courageously. We should have integrity, we should act sincerely, be compassionate and understanding. Though the world around us be not to our liking we shall have created for ourselves and our children an island of positivism—we shall have created "the world we want."

PREMIER NIKITA KHRUSHCHEV

## *Greatest Monkey or Greatest Man?*

Hitler and his cohorts were the greatest monkeys the world has ever known. By Premier Khrushchev's own testimony his predecessor was not too far behind Hitler in attaining that distinction.

I like Premier Khrushchev and believe he has made great strides in behalf of peace. But I like his wife, Nina, even more because in her face I see reflected the Eleanor Roosevelt of the Communist world. I believe she is good through and through, and for that reason I am sending her this open letter:

*Dear Mrs. Khrushchev,*

*If you had read my book you would know that I am not one of those "me and mine" types who feels that all is wrong with the other fellow and all is right with me. You would know that I do not believe the United States is perfect and that Russia is imperfect. You would have read of my contempt for most capitalists, my recognition that free enterprise is too often "me" enterprise. You would have read that it is my opinion that children in the Soviet Union receive a better education than our children today.*

*Objectivity, TRUTH is my god. I believe you are a noble woman with love and understanding for your fellow man. I believe if you and Mrs. Roosevelt had been given the decision to make, we would now have peace and brotherhood in this world.*

*I would remind you that men at your husband's age and mine must not put off for tomorrow what can be done today. We never know when the Grim Reaper will call our numbers. May your husband live to one hundred and twenty, but let him act as if he were to die tomorrow. If he passed away now he would be considered less than a man because of a terrible thing he has done.*

*I refer to his being the champion of the Arabs and providing them with the material and morale to perpetuate their forty million as monkeys instead of helping them develop into men. They do not let a day pass without threatening to slaughter and wipe off the face of the earth the two million Jews in Israel.*

*Consider the injustice of it. The two million people, easily one of the most productive for good on the face of the earth, are threatened by the forty million shiftless Arabs. It's bad enough that powerful nations stand by, but what about the Soviet Union that has armed and trained the Arabs?*

*Now, if you talk it over with Premier Khrushchev and show him the error of his ways, he, I hope and believe, would use his power and influence to bring about peace between Arab and Jew. That would be the most formidable move in the direction of world peace.*

*Though I believe the Premier has reason to feel hostile to the Germans because of the destruction they brought about to your land and people, I hope he will recognize that returning good for evil is the way of all great men and is necessary for creation of peace.*

*But in heaven's name, what has he against the Jews? That some of them are thieves in industry? The wonder is that there is a single honest man among them considering the treatment they have had from the majority for over two thousand years. In your own country check on the doctors, engineers, scientists, and you will find ten times more Jews in relation to population than others. Even as Oppenheimer and Teller with Einstein's inspiration built our hydrogen bomb, so you will find that Jews were responsible for helping your country achieve power.*

*In the history of time no group so small has done so much for all as have the Jews. With all their human faults they still represent, in relation to their numbers, the most productive force on earth for the betterment of mankind.*

*I plead with you, Mrs. Khrushchev, to be guided by that great big heart of yours. Talk it over with the Premier tonight.*

*When the announcement is made that he has ordered Nasser to create peace with Israel, he will at that moment insure his place as the greatest man in the world.*

*Sincerely and hopefully,*

*P.S.*

*I visited Russia in 1960. I hope you invite me to visit your country again when peace exists between Arab and Jew.*

THE RELIGIOUS-DEMOCRATIC IDEAL

## *I Have Faith in America*

I believe in America! I feel certain that we will not repeat the mistakes of those nations who departed from the ways of God. The great difference between us and the others is the fact that they were not born and bred democracies.

America was founded by men of vision and ideals. They were prophet rather than profit-minded. They thought in terms of the soul rather than the gold standard. Our founding fathers believed in the common man.

To get freedom they had to revolt. Now the people may get what they want by the vote.

Indeed, no nation in history was ever so blessed as was the United States of America when it was begotten on the religious democratic ideal.

That's why I believe America will withstand any storm or upheaval. Ours is not a behavior based on policy. Ours is a way of life based on prophecy.

*America is an idea! America symbolizes the religious democratic ideal. That's why I have faith in America!*

*I have faith in America.*
*Not because she has the highest mountains, for Mt. Everest in India is higher than Pike's Peak.*

*I have faith in America.*
*Not because she has the longest rivers. For the Nile is longer than the Mississippi.*

*I have faith in America.*
*Not because she has the loveliest lakes. For Lake Como in Switzerland is out of this world.*

*I have faith in America.*

*Not because its cities have the tallest buildings. Not because its people drive more automobiles. Not because Americans own more radios, washing machines, vacuum cleaners, bath tubs, telephones or most anything and everything that helps make living more comfortable and pleasant.*

*I have faith in America.*

*Not because of anything material!*

*I have faith in America.*

*Because of reasons spiritual!*

*I have faith in America.*

*Because of the religious democratic ideal which alone has made her great and has made her the hope of mankind.*

*I have faith in America.*

*Because of the religious democratic ideal which significantly reveals itself in the first three words of our preamble—"We the people . . ."*

*I have faith in America.*

*Because of the religious democratic ideal which is embodied in the Declaration of Independence and contains the most important words known to men—"All men are created equal."*

*I have faith in America.*

*Because of the religious democratic ideal which inspired Washington to say to the Jews of his day—"There shall be none to make you afraid."*

*I have faith in America.*

*Because of the religious democratic ideal which inspired a Patrick Henry to say—"Give me liberty or give me death."*

*I have faith in America.*

*Because of the religious democratic ideal which inspired Lincoln to say—". . . government of the people, by the people, for the people."*

*I have faith in America.*

*Because of the religious democratic ideal which inspired Franklin Delano Roosevelt to say—"We have nothing to fear but fear itself."*

*I have faith in America.*

*Because of the religious democratic ideal which inspired Wendell Willkie to make articulate to mankind the fact of "One World."*

*I have faith in America.*

*Because of the religious democratic ideal which inspired Henry Wallace to give hope to the meek and downtrodden by telling them that "One World" belonged to the common man.*

*I have faith in America.*

*Because of the religious democratic ideal which manifests itself in the reverence for God the Father, as all His children live together in peace and fellowship, be they Smiths, Johnsons, Fergusons, Cohens, Kellys, Rizzos, Schmidts, Ytangs, Svobodas.*

*I have faith in America.*

*Because of the religious democratic ideal which gives promise of ushering in God's Kingdom on earth wherein all will love their neighbors.*

I pray to God that Americans will never be treasonable to their heritage and deviate in the slightest from the religious democratic ideal on which our nation was founded and which is incorporated in the Declaration of Independence, the Constitution and the Bill of Rights.

Let us remember why we inherited an America more perfect than any other nation on earth.

Let us understand why we presently have an America that is yet the hope of all the nations.

Let us resolve to consecrate ourselves to the religious democratic ideal so that America will fulfill its destiny of leading "One World" into becoming the spiritual abode of One People worshipping at the altar of One God.

GOD

## *Let Us Try to Understand Him*

Abraham discovered God. Legend says it came about in this way. All human beings worshipped idols and his father had a shop where they were sold. One day by accident Abraham bumped into some idols and they broke into many pieces. This startled him. "If I am more powerful than the idols it is silly for me to worship them," he mused to himself. After much thought and deliberation Abraham concluded that there is a Spiritual Force that governs the universe. That Force which we know as God is too powerful and complex for the human mind to envision. God is Spirit and more powerful than all men, potentates and other forces combined. He governs the universe. Abraham perceived that God was ONE; that He created the world and all other planets; that He was eternal and that none could compare with Him.

That is how it came to pass that Abraham was the first Jew. Those who accepted his point of view and ceased worshipping idols came to be known as Jews. All other people were called gentiles. Generations afterward the Jewish prophet Moses received from God the Ten Commandments on top of Mount Sinai. Subsequently, with the inspiration from God and dedication to his will, the Jews created the holy book . . . the Bible. It begins with the story of creation and tells the history of the Jewish people almost to the time of Jesus.

The Jews conceived and created prayers to worship this Spirit that governed the universe. The single most important prayer among Jews is the one that exclaims: "Hear, O Israel, the Lord is our God, the Lord is One."

Christianity emerged from Judaism. Jesus Christ, his disciples and his biographers Paul, Mark, Luke and John were all Jewish. Therefore they all believed in the God of Abraham. As a matter of fact Jesus worshipped only in Jewish synagogues.

Christianity, however, holds the view that Jesus Christ is the son of God and appeared on earth to live and die to fulfill God's mission. Christians believe Jesus was born as an ordinary mortal, but was conceived through immaculate conception. Also Christians believe in the Holy Ghost. The term Trinity refers to God the Father, Jesus the Son and the Holy Ghost. One Christian sect called Unitarian does not believe in the Holy Ghost or the divinity of Jesus. Hence the name Unitarian.

There are a great variety of other religions practiced by the tremendous population that comprises India, China, Japan and other peoples of central and eastern Asia. Buddha and Confucius are venerated by hundreds of millions in the Orient.

In the Middle East where most Arab countries are situated the people worship Allah as their God. There are, however, many who believe in Christianity as in the case of Lebanon where a large percentage of Lebanese are Christians. Most Moslems worship God and venerate Mohammed as their greatest prophet.

China has the largest population in the world. Today it is Red. There are many millions who are still devoted to Confucianism. However, the government officially expects its citizens to be atheists. Together with all other Communist nations there are over one billion people in the world committed to atheism.

Happily, it is not necessary that people have the same religious beliefs in order to get along with one another. There are families where its members worship different faiths and still others that are atheists. They get along fine because they minimize their differences and magnify the verities they hold in common.

Robert Ingersoll was the foremost atheist in America. At his grave were assembled the foremost clergymen of his time. They came to pay homage to a man they considered as profoundly "religious" as anyone could be. They all felt Ingersoll was as fine a person as ever lived. After all, atheists do not approve of murder, theft and any behaviour that is immoral or unethical.

Surely God is little concerned with what people say, but greatly interested in what they do. I am sure that is what Jesus had in mind in saying, "Not those of ye who hold onto my cloak and cry Lord, Lord . . . but those of ye who act righteously will enter the kingdom of heaven." He emphasized that action speaks louder than words.

There are two children in a family. One lives at home and the other in a far distant place. The one at home uses dope and for many reasons has been in and out of jail. He repents, goes to church frequently and prays a lot. Yet he is a source of aggravation to his parents. Thousands of miles away the atheist son lives a wholesome life and is a source of joy to his father and mother. Whom do the parents appreciate more?

Dare we assume God is less perceptive and understanding?

Is God a Baptist, Methodist, Mormon, Jew or Catholic? Is God a Buddhist or Mohammedan? What kind of God do we worship?

Does He prefer tall to short people?

Does He like white better than black?

Does He care about one's looks?

Does He favor your church?

Does He concern Himself with what you have or what you give?

Does He admire the rich, the powerful, the brilliant, or does He care as much for the poor, the weak and the simple-minded?

Does He pay homage to celebrities?

Does He reward with good health or great wealth the doer of good deeds or with His greatest gift, peace of mind?

Does He take cognizance of lofty words or kind acts?

Does He bless your country, your leaders, your people more than others?

Does He play favorites with His children?

The religion we are born into is a matter of accident. The country of our birth too is accidental. Had we been born into a different religion we probably would be loyal to it. Had we been born in Brazil we would be Brazillians. In Cuba? We would be Cubans. It does not behoove us to be arbitrary or dogmatic, but rather shouldn't we be tolerant and understanding of other faiths and nationalities?

When we do worthy deeds we become partners with God. God helps those that help themselves. This story will illustrate:

Rastus, a colored man in Alabama, had a farm that was the wonder of the state. Everyone talked about it.

One Sunday the visiting bishop in the church remarked after the services, "Oh, yes . . . I just remembered, this is the town nearby that fabulous farm I've heard so much about. I must see it." Rastus stepped up and invited the bishop for Sunday dinner.

Afterward the bishop joined Rastus on the back porch where they could see the sloping miracle. The bishop beheld what appeared as a multi-colored checker board . . . in viewing the fantastic farm. He was struck by the beauty and the grandeur of this showplace. Finally he found the words to express his amazement. "Rastus, I want you to know that you and the Lord performed a miracle on this land." To which Rastus meekly replied, "Bishop, I wish you could have seen this place when the Lord had it all to Himself."

God expects the initiative to come from us. Being the Supreme Father He will naturally help those of His children who cannot help themselves.

I have not tried to make a case for atheism or any religious group. I seek to make a case for brotherhood. I do want people to begin to know themselves, to check on their beliefs and to consider whether their worship of God is genuine or lip service. I pray that we understand the childishness in praying to God for things we want and the maturity of telling Him what we aspire to do for Him.

Speaking for myself I know that without God I am nothing. With God I am quite a person. In the writing of this book I have often turned to my wife and said, "I pushed the pencil, but God dictated." Out of nowhere ideas came to me without any deliberation or effort on my part. Isn't that God inspired?

Readers can sense that I am a well adjusted and happy human being. I am nevertheless troubled by the fact that people hate, are petty, narrow and lacking in understanding. I believe this is due to the magnification of differences and minimization of things we have in common. In the meantime the hydrogen bombs tick ominously on. Before it is too late we must get together.

This calls to mind the story of the farming community in search of a missing child. Many hours had passed with hundreds looking here, there and everywhere without locating him. Finally, a child suggested that it might be a good idea for them to get together and form a gigantic circle . . . each about five yards apart. Then they were to come inward to a central spot. In that way they would probably find the child. This they did and coming close in they found the child . . . dead. The parents rushed to the scene and the father cradled the child in his arms. Finally these words came from him as he questioned the mute crowd, "Why did we run about like monkeys? Why didn't we act like men and get together sooner?"

Mankind must learn that togetherness with love will keep us alive and happy. With the vast storehouse of hydrogen bombs that exist we can no longer afford the luxury of one group considering itself superior to another. How long will the policy of Apartheid continue in South Africa? How much longer will some Americans hold onto the philosophy that dark skinned people are inferior?

I have taught my children that they will never meet people that are inferior to them. By the same token they will not find people superior to them. The prophet Malachi summed up the matter in saying, "Have we not all one Father? Hath not one God created us?"

When we understand God we will find ourselves adhering to the prophet Micha's admonition, "Do justice, love mercy and walk humbly with thy God."

WHAT HAVE I LEARNED AND ACCOMPLISHED?

## *Where Will It Lead?*

I learned that one cannot live by bread alone. That after achieving security for his family, one should dedicate oneself to helping others.

I learned that education is a never-ending process. Formal education is only the foundation for study and learning that should continue throughout one's life.

To seek perfection in oneself or to expect it in others is unreasonable, but striving for perfection should be the aspiration for all human beings.

I have tried to set an example for my children, my business associates, my friends and neighbors. Practically every category of charitable cause has been the recipient of aid from our Foundation in relation to our ability to give. We have supported all kinds of hospitals. We have given to the widow and orphan, the sick and maimed, the blind, the mute, the retarded, to cerebral palsy, muscular dystrophy, asthma. We have given to the cause closest to my heart, the United Jewish Appeal, almost three quarters of a million dollars.

Politically we have supported the organizations that strive to improve the lot of the masses. I will never vote for the candidate who represents the vested interests first and the people second.

I am proud of the slogan I coined, "Do business on Monday in the spirit of Sunday." I hope to see it become widely popular.

One of the greatest sources of satisfaction to me has been the establishment of the GOOD HEART AWARD. I pray some day to have it exist in every country of the world.

Two other projects I hope to dedicate myself to: First, to seek wide dissemination of this book in the hope that people will distinguish between the purely physical human being . . . the monkey, and the spiritual one who has elevated himself into being a man; second, it is my desire to have children throughout the world pledge allegiance to the flag of one world. The simple pledge I conceived of goes:

> *I pledge allegiance to the flag of one world and to the humanity for which it stands. One people, living in one world worshipping one God."*

I leave my children a good heritage. My charity foundation and, I hope, my spiritually creative ideas will serve to give purpose and direction to them and their children.

At sixty-one years of age, with a medical history such as I have, I hardly expect to live the years needed to complete my projects. Friends have intimated that my two coronaries came about because of my relentless desire to change the complexion of the universe. I am thrilled that there is some truth in this observation. I hope and pray that when I am called to my Maker my children will be able to utter the words of an unknown author that I treasure above all:

> *"He wore himself out in the pursuit of worthy, even though unattainable ends, but in so doing learned of ecstasy in living."*